Crisis
Management

Harvard Business Essentials

The New Manager's Guide and Mentor

The Harvard Business Essentials series is designed to provide comprehensive advice, personal coaching, background information, and guidance on the most relevant topics in business. Drawing on rich content from Harvard Business School Publishing and other sources, these concise guides are carefully crafted to provide a highly practical resource for readers with all levels of experience and will prove especially valuable for the new manager. To assure quality and accuracy, each volume is closely reviewed by a specialized content adviser from a world-class business school. Whether you are a new manager seeking to expand your skills or a seasoned professional looking to broaden your knowledge base, these solution-oriented books put reliable answers at your fingertips.

Other books in the series:

Finance for Managers
Hiring and Keeping the Best People
Managing Change and Transition
Negotiation
Business Communication
Managing Projects Large and Small
Manager's Toolkit

Crisis Management

Master the Skills to
Prevent Disasters

Harvard Business School Press | *Boston, Massachusetts*

Library of Congress Cataloging-in-Publication Data
Harvard business essentials: crisis managment.
    p.   cm.—(The Harvard business essentials series)
Includes bibliographical references and index.
ISBN 1-59139-437-6
1. Crisis management. I. Title: Managing crisis.
II. Harvard Business School. III. Series.
HD49.H367 2004
658.4'056—dc22

                                                    2004002700

Contents

Crisis Management

Introduction

On February 1, 2003, the space shuttle *Columbia* and its seven-person crew was reentering the Earth's atmosphere and navigating toward a touchdown at Edwards Air Force Base in California. Its fifteen days in orbit had been productive and uneventful. The crew had conducted eighty-plus experiments, many having to do with the application of microgravity. But the mission was now over, and the great craft was streaking home. With only twenty minutes left in the mission, everything was proceeding according to plan.

Next to takeoff, atmospheric reentry has always been the most perilous stage of space exploration. After hurdling through the vacuum of space at speeds in excess of 17,000 miles per hour, a spacecraft plunges by degrees into the soupy atmosphere, creating heat-producing friction and subjecting the craft to tremendous stress. U.S. shuttle vehicles depend on heat-shielding materials and the piloting skills of their commanders to handle those two perils and to descend safely. But on that day in February something went terribly wrong. *Columbia* disintegrated like a meteor as it entered the atmosphere, killing its crew and shocking millions around the globe.

What went wrong—and why? Those were questions addressed by the Columbia Accident Investigation Board. Seven months after the tragedy, the board released its findings, which were highly critical of the National Aeronautical and Space Administration (NASA), which ran the shuttle program. The board traced the cause of the accident to a piece of insulation material on the boost rocket. During the launch, a chunk of that insulation broke free, striking and damaging heat-resistant tiles on the leading edge of *Columbia*'s left wing.

During reentry, high heat was able to enter the wing structure at the point of damage, eventually melting the wing's supporting structures, and causing the craft to tumble out of control. With control lost, reentry heat and stresses broke *Columbia* into pieces.

That was the physical cause of the accident. But how was it allowed to happen? Behind the physical cause of *Columbia's* destruction the board detected an organizational flaw that made the accident possible—if not inevitable. Its report concluded that NASA's organizational culture was as much at fault as the piece of foam that delivered the fatal blow to the wing's protective tiles. In its view, the organizational causes of the accident were rooted in the shuttle program's history and culture, including years of resource constraints, fluctuating priorities, schedule pressures, and lack of a national vision for human space flight. It found that NASA's culture and practices were detrimental to safety. These included a reliance on past success as a substitute for sound engineering, organizational barriers to the communication of critical safety information, and stifled professional differences of opinion.[1] In particular, its investigation board pointed to attitudes that were "incompatible with an organization that deals with high-risk technology."[2]

More damning, investigators concluded that the shuttle program's structure and processes, and therefore the managers in charge, resisted new information of the type that could have prevented the disaster. They also failed to develop simple contingency plans for a reentry emergency. "They were convinced, without study, that nothing could be done about such an emergency. The intellectual curiosity and skepticism that a solid safety culture requires was almost entirely absent."[3]

The *Columbia* disaster was a serious blow to NASA and to its shuttle program. The lives of seven astronauts and a multibillion-dollar space vehicle had been lost. Upcoming shuttle missions had to be grounded until *Columbia's* sister spacecraft could be certified as safe to fly. Together these threw a monkey wrench into the NASA timetable for space exploration. And because the shuttle was the principal vehicle for resupply of the International Space Station, that program was equally threatened.

Perhaps worse, employee morale was shaken, and NASA's reputation for excellence and competence was badly tarnished. The public no longer viewed it as the can-do organization whose feats in space thrilled the world during the 1960s and 1970s. Given the *Columbia* tragedy and the critical judgment of the investigation board, would public support for NASA's mission dwindle? Would Congress reduce future funding? How would NASA management face up to its crisis? Could it possibly resolve the problem?

Crises afflict more than high-risk organizations such as NASA. Every organization is subject to crisis, whether it realizes it or not. Consider the following examples:

- Government regulators discover that some employees of a leading mutual fund company had been indulging in illegal trading activities—activities that reduced the returns of shareholders. Within just a few weeks of this revelation, individual investors and pension funds have withdrawn billion of dollars from the fund company, threatening its future existence.

- A tanker runs aground, spilling more than two hundred fifty thousand barrels of oil into the waters of a pristine Alaskan estuary. Fines and clean-up bills pour in—so do lawsuits and letters from outraged customers and shareholders.

- A portfolio manager tries to produce a higher yield for money market fund shareholders through the use of speculative derivatives; no one notices. When the derivatives unravel, investors—including many charities and arts institutions—lose 25 percent of their money. And the company loses the goodwill and community trust it spent decades building.

- Two days after his high-tech company made its initial public offering of shares, the CEO/founder—and the real brains of the high-tech start-up company—is killed in a traffic accident. Employees and investors ask themselves, "What's left of this company?"

- Millions of Americans watched a television documentary in which an automaker's vehicle was shown bursting into flames during a simulated crash. Many are outraged and vow to never again purchase a car or truck from that company. A month later, the company revealed proof that the documentary's producers rigged the crash so that fire would result. But the truth has little effect on public opinion; the damage to the company and its reputation is already done.

Each of the anecdotes just cited involved a real company in a real crisis. Do you recognize any of them? Could something like those situations happen to your company?

A *crisis* is a change—either sudden or evolving—that results in an urgent problem that must be addressed immediately. For a business, a crisis is anything with the potential to cause sudden and serious damage to it employees, reputation, or bottom line.

A major crisis will affect the entire organization and, in some cases, such as those of Enron and Barings Bank, can lead to its collapse. Managers whose organizations are in the midst of a crisis must act quickly to recognize its source, contain it, and eventually resolve the crisis with the least amount of damage. In this sense crisis management is part of a larger system of organizational risk management that includes diversification and insurance. And though every reader can surely recall a crisis situation at his or another organization, few managers actively plan for potential crises. Fewer still receive training in crisis management. Neither of those deficiencies should surprise us because crisis management as a formal field of study and training is relatively new, only emerging over the past three decades. This book aims to remedy this situation by explaining the essentials of crisis management. It will not make you an expert, but it will give you a practical framework for coming to grips with and mastering an unplanned and unanticipated damaging event.

What's Ahead

Have you ever stopped to think of the many things that could go wrong for your company? Some crises are caused by acts of nature: a paralyzing blizzard, an earthquake, or a flood. Others stem from acts of human malice or criminal behavior: the emotionally disturbed employee who comes to the office with a grudge to settle, or the trusted financial officer secretly conspiring to dodge the company's legal tax obligations. The sources of potential organizational crises are many. Chapter 1 reviews the usual sources and offers a practical and systematic method you can use to identify the ones most likely to affect your company—in effect, a risk audit. It will help you prioritize those risks in terms of their potential monetary impact and the probability of their occurrence.

Once you've developed a crisis risk audit and prioritized its elements, you'll be ready for the next step, which is risk avoidance. As chapter 2 explains, managers practice crisis avoidance all the time, usually without even thinking about it. Crisis avoidance can be as mundane as the internal financial controls that prevent embezzlement or as complex as the design that makes it next to impossible for a purchaser to injure herself when using a company's new food chopper. This chapter offers a method that you and your colleagues can use to systematically search for ways to avoid crises associated with items in your crisis risk audit. The method requires that you compare the cost of avoiding the risk with the likely cost that the risk would inflict. By comparing the potential cost of a crisis with the cost of avoiding it, you'll be in a better position to make a decision about how you'll allocate scarce resources.

Chapter 3 is on contingency planning, or preparing today for tomorrow's potential setbacks. Contingency planning involves organizing and making as many decisions as possible *before* a crisis occurs, when there is more time to consider options and no pressure or panic. Contingency plans are not designed to prevent crises, but they can lessen the damage of crises and return situations to normal more quickly. This chapter offers a five-step program for contingency planning: organizing the planning team, assessing the scope of the problem, developing a plan, testing the plan, and keeping the plan up-to-date. Develop contingency plans for each serious unavoidable risk, and you'll be more likely to weather a future crisis.

Chapter 4 will help you recognize a crisis situation before it is out of control. Some crises are self-evident: You get a call in the night that your finished-goods warehouse is ablaze and likely to burn to the ground. There's no mistaking that crisis. Others are less obvious. For example, female employees may have been complaining among each other about the inappropriate behavior of their male boss, but none has said anything to the human resource department. There are rumors about this situation but nothing concrete— and no one is checking the rumors.

Some crises are like fire. They start small in some unobserved area. If you smell the smoke and catch the fire early, you will avert a major crisis. Left untended, these smoldering problems may grow into catastrophic infernos. Are you hearing persistent rumors about a manager who hasn't been playing by the rules? Has the company fired or ignored an employee who keeps complaining about safety problems? Do your instincts tell you that there's something wrong here? Chapter 4 is about crisis recognition. It will alert you to the early signals of impeding trouble and explain why so many of them pass unnoticed. Better still, this chapter offers practical advice for making your organization more attuned to crisis warning signs.

Once a crisis management team recognizes a problem, the group's first responsibility is to contain it before it has time to grow worse. Chapter 5 urges crisis managers to act quickly and decisively, to put people first, to be visibly on the scene, and to communicate liberally. Those actions will help contain the crisis. True, acting quickly and decisively is more easily said than done. Facts are often few in the early stages of crisis. But sitting and waiting for all the information to be gathered and processed will give the crisis time to grow. So what should managers do? The chapter advises them to fall back on their training and planning when the situation is murky. They should also allow their values and best instincts to guide them.

Crisis resolution is the subject of chapter 6. Fast and effective action on the containment front will result in a crisis that is smaller and more manageable than it would be otherwise. From that point, the job of the crisis management team is to keep on top of the problem and not to let up until it is resolved and the situation has returned to normal. Again, quick action and communication are recommended. In some cases, as in the aftermath of a natural disaster, a crisis management team will find the tools of project management extremely useful in resolving its problem. As explained in this chapter, crises and projects have many common elements. For example, both are nonroutine, rarely repeating activities, and they require the skills and experience of people from many different functions. The main phases of project management are explained in the context of crisis resolution.

The media—newspapers, television, and radio—represent a special communication challenge to crisis managers, one that few businesspeople are trained to handle. Approached wisely, the media may carry your story as you want it framed. Mishandle the media, on the other hand, and your company may be publicly skewered. Chapter 7 offers advice about dealing with the media. In addition, it recommends that you identify the different segments of your audience and craft appropriate messages for each. This is what your company does when it communicates with the marketplace of customers, and you should do the same in communicating with your various stakeholders: employees, customers, suppliers, investors, community leaders, and so forth. Further, the chapter recommends that you channel your segmented messages through the appropriate media.

The final chapter is about learning. Every crisis is costly. Even if you resolve your crisis effectively and with a high degree of professionalism, there are bound to be costs in terms of money, time, morale, and public image. Given those costs, you might as well get something in return. Smart organizations learn from every experience and apply that learning to future challenges. Learning makes them wiser and more effective. This chapter provides useful tips on closing down a crisis team and how you can use its learning to avoid and/or prepare for subsequent crises.

Once you've finished reading these chapters you'll find some supplementary sections: two appendixes and a list of books and articles you may want to consult as you expand your knowledge of crisis management. The appendixes contain the following:

- An emergency contact list of people and phone numbers; complete this list and keep it handy in anticipation of future crises—and make sure it's up-to-date

- A checklist of "30 Warning Signs of Potential Trouble"

- A useful worksheet for capturing the lessons learned in a crisis

- A primer on writing an effective press release

The section titled "For Further Reading" contains references to recent books and articles—many of them classics—that provide either much more material or unique insights into the topics covered here. If you'd like to learn more about any of the topics we've included in the book, these references will help you. In addition, the official Harvard Business Essentials Web site, www.elearning.hbsp.org/businesstools, offers free interactive versions of tools, checklists, and worksheets cited in this book and other books in the Harvard Business Essentials series.

The content of this book is greatly informed by a number of sources, in particular the Crisis Management module of Harvard ManageMentor®, an online service of Harvard Business School Publishing.

1

Taking Stock of Potential Perils

What Could Go Wrong?

Key Topics Covered in This Chapter

- *Major sources of potential crises*

- *Systematically auditing crisis risk*

- *A practical method for evaluating different risks*

CRISIS MANAGEMENT ideally begins before a crisis actually occurs—in a calm and objective environment. It begins with a thorough audit of organizational risks and identification of those that could result in major problems. This chapter will explain how to conduct such an audit and provide a method you can use to prioritize the risks that represent the greatest potential—and probability—for trouble. But first, let's consider major sources of potential crises.

Sources of Potential Crises

It would be impossible to list every potential business crisis, but understanding some major categories of risk can help you identify the types of crises you and your organization need to avoid (if possible) and for which you should prepare. Many risks are determined by the company's unique business. For example, a medical device manufacturer may be acutely at risk for product liability suits resulting from injuries or damaging side effects experienced by users of its devices. Do you remember Robbins, maker of the Dalkin Shield intrauterine birth control device? Robbins no longer exists. A sea of personal injury lawsuits drove it into bankruptcy.

Many companies have learned through experience to keep a very close eye on particular industry-related sources of risk and to develop plans for handling them. Consider these:

- **Major airlines.** Statistically, a passenger traveling on a major air carrier is safer than on just about any other form of transportation. Nevertheless, a single crash is generally catastrophic. Recognizing such vulnerability, all major airlines focus on the possibility of crashes, how to prevent them, and how to address the aftermath. Most are well prepared to deal with hijackings as well.

- **Chemical and petroleum companies.** These companies must always be on guard against the possibility of explosions and the discharge of polluting or toxic materials into the environment. Any such event could create a serious crisis.

- **Food processors and packers.** Today's high-volume processing of meat, dairy products, and other foods means that huge amounts of tainted and potentially deadly products can be quickly distributed over a wide geographic area and do their mischief before any problem is identified. This is what happened in 2001 when IBP, Inc., the world's largest beef producer, had to recall 566,000 pounds of beef—a single day's production—contaminated with E. coli. By the time the recall was announced, the meat had been distributed in thirty-one U.S. states, and much of it had been consumed by unwitting customers. Producers at the farm level are at even greater risk of catastrophe, as the United Kingdom's experience with mad cow and hoof-and-mouth disease demonstrated. Those outbreaks resulted in financial ruin for many producers and devastated agricultural communities.

- **Financial services companies.** Securities broker-dealers have a long history of public relations embarrassments and crises in customer confidence. Most are caused by inappropriate investment recommendations by individual stockbrokers. These are generally settled through arbitration. More damaging cases stem from a failure of broker-dealers to perform due diligence on the investments they encourage their representatives to recommend to customers. In the 1980s, for example, dozens of U.S. broker-dealers were promoting interest-paying annuities issued by an insurance company that was later found to be incapable of backing its commitments. The fact that these dealers promoted the annuities as safe investments, suitable for retirees and other risk-averse clients, compounded the consequences, and they ended up refunding hundreds of millions of dollars to damaged customers.

What are your company's greatest areas of vulnerability? Is anyone addressing them?

Accidents and Natural Events

An accident or natural event of catastrophic magnitude can strike unexpectedly—whether it's an earthquake, typhoon, tornado, hurricane, blizzard, flood, fire, or some other disaster. And don't think that it couldn't happen to you. Businesses located in downtown Chicago never thought about flood risk until a freak accident inundated their basements in early 1992, knocking out power, water, and heating/cooling systems. The flooding began when workers who were installing new pilings punched a car-sized hole through the bottom of the channelized Chicago River, a tame waterway that meanders placidly through the city's downtown. That hole emptied into an abandoned rail tunnel, which quickly flooded, sending river water into the basements of major buildings in the Windy City's core business district. Lacking power, utilities, and clean water, thousands of offices had to shut their doors for three to four days, causing losses estimated at $1.95 billion.

The impact of accidents and natural events can also be felt indirectly. Because of supply-chain linkages, a fire or flood somewhere else in the world can create a crisis here at home. For example, a total-loss fire at a battery-manufacturing plant in Japan had a profound impact on Motorola, which relied solely on the Japanese plant to supply a unique battery. That fire set back Motorola's production of some items for five months.[1]

Health and Environmental Disasters

Unlike natural events, some health- and environment-related disasters, though not necessarily *caused* by a company, are directly related to it. The company is responsible—or is perceived to be responsible—for dealing with them. Consider the following examples:

- **Product tampering.** Interference by an outsider can harm consumers and affect the overall image of your product and company. This is what happened to Johnson & Johnson in the infamous Tylenol case. Several people were poisoned in October 1982 when an outsider inserted cyanide-laced capsules into a number of bottles containing the popular painkiller. Johnson & Johnson reacted quickly and effectively in this crisis, recalling all Tylenol products and replacing them with tamper-proof packaging. Though the company didn't cause any deaths or injuries, it nevertheless paid a huge price. Total loss from the product recall, development of the new packaging, and lost sales may have exceeded $1 billion.

- **Catastrophic accidents.** These are expensive to fix and cause real damage to people. And the lawsuits that result can cause unfavorable media coverage of the company for years. The plant explosion that occurred at Union Carbide's chemical plant in Bhopal, India, in 1984 is probably the worst of these catastrophes in recent times, based simply on deaths and injuries (an estimated seven thousand were killed, and an even greater number were injured). The 1986 meltdown of the Chernobyl nuclear plant in the old Soviet Union runs a close second. The full costs of these tragic accidents—to the companies and the victims—is beyond calculation.

- **Environmental harm.** The industrialized world has come a long way in its understanding of the environment and the adverse impacts of many human activities on it. Many companies have taken positive steps to eliminate or minimize the possible environmental consequences of their activities. Others blithely conduct business as usual until fines and public censure hit them over the head. Still other companies are paying today for the deeds of a previous generation of managers, even though those deeds may not have been illegal at the time. General Electric's (GE) continuing problem in the upper Hudson River in New York State is a prime example. GE used PCBs (chlorinated hydrocarbons) many decades ago in the manufacture of transformers and other electrical equipment at its plants along the Hudson. Large quantities of the substance found their way to the river and its bottom sediment. As knowledge of the health effects of PCBs became better known in the 1970s, their manufacture and use were banned in the United States. GE complied, but PCBs remained in the river sediment near its plants. The result has been a long history of litigation, health studies, and, more recently, plans for costly dredging and remediation of portions of the Hudson River.

Technological Breakdowns

Remember the Great Blackout of 2003? A glitch in the U.S. electrical grid knocked out power in a huge swath stretching from New York City to the Midwest. At this writing, the damages were still being tallied. Similar incidents struck Italy and Norway in 2003.

Technical breakdowns that happen on a grand scale also happen on a small scale to individual businesses. Everyone knows what it's like when the company server goes down. You cannot send or receive e-mail. Access to your databases evaporates. Customers cannot place orders on your Web site. Short interruptions, of course, rarely constitute a crisis. But some do. For example, back in February 2000, cyberpranksters launched the first major attack of the Internet Age. Their targets included Yahoo!, Amazon.com, eBay, CNN, and E*Trade—the biggest of the big online operators. The weapon in this case was a "denial of service" attack in which attackers bombard a target's servers with thousands of hits.

The community of auction buyers and sellers on eBay was hard hit by the attack. The sellers whose auctions were closing that day

Backup Capacity Helps

Though damaged by the cyberattack of February 2000, eBay suffered less than most other target sites. As described by authors David Bunnell and Richard Luecke: "eBay's problems . . . were actually less severe than they might have been, thanks to the company's long-term plan to scale up its computer infrastructure. [It] had invested an estimated $30 million in backup servers and other equipment, with the aim of ensuring substantial excess capacity. . . . [That] added capacity dampened the blow." The popular auction site still had to make amends with sellers whose auctions had been disrupted. And it had to assure its community of users that it was taking steps to prevent a recurrence. The extra capacity of its infrastructure, however, made the event something less than a real crisis.

SOURCE: David Bunnell with Richard Luecke, *The eBay Phenomenon* (New York: John Wiley & Sons, Inc., 2000), 151.

found few bidders. It's not that bidders weren't out there; they simply couldn't get through to make their final offers. The cost to eBay and to thousands of sellers was high.

The crisis potential of technical breakdowns grows as businesses become more dependent on computers to communicate, store information, conduct research, buy, and sell. Many today could not function without their brainy machines and software. But computing and telecommunications power makes these same companies highly vulnerable to data loss, security breaches, malicious hacking, and ordinary equipment breakdowns.

Where are your company's technology vulnerabilities? Has anyone taken steps to find and protect them?

Economic and Market Forces

Stockbrokers and economists like to say, "A rising tide lifts all boats," which is a way of saying that all (or most) businesses do well during good economic times. The reverse of that saying is, "When the tide goes out, all the boats go down." Stock prices tend to tumble together—even the prices of companies that are doing very well.

Indeed, the fortunes of all businesses are to some extent bound to the ups and downs of the economic cycle. Down phases are particularly dangerous for companies with high fixed costs—prominent examples include manufacturers with inflexible labor contracts and heavy investments in plants and equipment. Their monthly bills stay high even as their revenue streams dry up during recessions, causing cash squeezes and, in some cases, subsequent business crises.

Some companies find themselves exposed to an in-favor/out-of-favor cycle. Biotech and dot-com companies are striking examples. Investors alternatively love them or scorn them. And these companies—which are mostly start-ups—depend on regular infusions of investor cash to stay alive. Consider this example:

> *A young biotech company doing stem cell research has a "burn rate" of $100,000 per month. It has $1.2 million in cash and no products ready for sale. This means that the company will need an infusion of cash from investors within twelve months.*

Is this a crisis? Not necessarily. If the biotech industry is in favor with investors, and if the company has a credible staff of scientists working toward a wonder cure of some commonplace affliction, more cash is likely to appear. If biotech is out of favor, however, investment capital will be hard to find. The company will head toward disaster. Once its cash is gone, it will implode.

If you've been with your company for a number of years, you understand how it is affected by the ups and downs of the business cycle. Does your chief financial officer have a plan to shore up the company's solvency during the down phases? Is the plan credible or tested?

Rogue Employees

All companies depend on people to get things done. And in an era characterized by wider spans of control and a greater need for speed and flexibility, they are giving employees greater discretion over decisions. Employee empowerment has generally been a good thing, unleashing personal ingenuity and effort that in the past was smothered beneath hierarchical controls. But empowerment has a downside. An employee acting without close supervision or consultation may throw the organization into crisis. Here are some examples:

- A big-city police captain turned a blind eye to the constant sexual harassment of his precinct's three female patrol officers. City policy forbade that kind of behavior, but the city also gave its precinct captains responsibility for enforcing policy. In this case, the policy was not being enforced. Fed up with their ill treatment, the three women brought a lawsuit against the captain, the department, and the city. They won a $900,000 settlement, and the entire police force got a black eye.

- In Boston's infamous pedophile scandal of 2001 to 2003, senior Catholic clerics routinely—and for years—had covered up the crimes of more than a dozen abusive priests. Their solution to complaints by lay members of the Church was to transfer errant priests to other parishes, where the priests sought out new victims. Revelation of these crimes and their concealment created a scandal that ended the career of the archbishop of Boston, cost $85 million to settle legal claims, and created a huge loss of respect for the Church.

Some industries go to great lengths to assure that an employee, or supervisor acting as agent of his company, does not create a legal or ethical breach. For example, register representatives (more generally known as stockbrokers) of securities firms are required to observe the first commandment of their industry: "Know thy customer." Prior to engaging in any transaction, a registered rep must inquire as to the customer's investment objective, knowledge of investing, income, net worth, and sensitivity to risk. The stocks, bonds, and other financial products recommended by the rep must be suitable in terms of those customer factors—that's the second commandment of the industry. Supervisors are required by stock exchange rules to monitor the transaction of each register representative to assure adherence to those two commandments. Furthermore, every firm must have a compliance department, whose sole purpose is to ensure that all transactions conform with government and exchange rules.

Yet despite regulation, training, and watchdog compliance departments, customer rip-offs have not been eliminated from the securities industry. Not a month passes without a report of some risk-averse widow being talked into investing her life savings in a risky portfolio of penny stocks and junk bonds, or whatever else pays a high commission to the registered rep. These violations seldom rise to the level of crisis for securities firms. But their revelations tarnish the image of trustworthiness and good stewardship on which individual brokerage firms depend. That was the experience of twelve major U.S. financial services companies in late 2002, when they agreed to pay a combined total of more than $1 billion in fines and legal settlements. The Securities and Exchange Commission and state regulators charged these firms with allowing conflicts of interest to color their stock recommendations to clients. Prosecutors revealed that star analysts were touting the stocks of various companies to investors even as they were privately denigrating these companies' future prospects. The reason for these mixed messages was a conflict of interest, which encouraged the analysts to recommend some stocks as a way of currying favor with the issuing companies, whose fee-rich investment banking business they sought.

Does your firm have any "loose cannon" employees acting as its agents? If it does, be on guard. Even if they are brilliant and bringing in the money, their methods may bring your firm into disrepute. And how about your managers and supervisors? Are they doing their jobs, or are they inclined to look the other way as long as their subordinates are producing results?

Events of nature, health and the environment, technology, market forces, and rogue employees have the potential to damage any and all of a company's most important assets: its people, its bottom line, and it reputation. They are not the only source of potential crises, but they must be considered when conducting a risk audit.

How One Rogue Employee Sank a Centuries-Old Bank

Barings Bank, founded in the eighteenth century, was a fixture in the British world of finance. It was also the bank of the British monarchy. Among its employees was a young trader named Nicholas Leeson, who worked in the Barings Singapore office. Leeson's bosses thought that he was arbitraging futures contracts—that is, trying to profit from price differences for the very same contracts in different markets, specifically, the Osaka Securities Exchange and Singapore International Monetary Exchange. Arbitrage is not generally a risky game. The trader buys contracts in one market and immediately sells them in another where the price is slightly higher. Though price differences between markets are usually small, the volumes traded by arbitrageurs are large, allowing a skillful operator to make a decent profit.

Unknown to his bosses back in London, however, Leeson was playing a more dangerous game, selling put and call options on the same futures contracts: a strategy known as a "straddle." Had the market remained stable, Leeson might have won his bets and made substantial money for the bank, but a disastrous earthquake in Kobe, Japan, created huge price fluctuations, which undermined his positions. Working frantically to avoid a loss, he increased his bets. Using a fraudulent account, he attempted to artificially lift the price of his contracts by buying them in huge quantities. That scheme failed, and horrendous losses followed. The venerable Barings Bank went out of business, and Nick Leeson went to prison.

Were Leeson's managers lax in monitoring his activities? Probably. Would closer supervision have identified his gamble before the damage was done? Maybe yes, maybe no. Trading tactics in futures and options exchanges are mind-bogglingly complex. And the fact that he used a fraudulent account might have hidden his game from even the closest scrutiny.

Identifying Potential Crises

Knowing where to look for potential crises is the first step in conducting a crisis audit. The next task is to look systematically within those sources to identify things that could lead to trouble in the future. Some will represent more costly risks than others. Some will have a higher probability of occurring. Don't be concerned about the magnitude and probability of different risks just yet. For the moment, just make a list of things that could lead to big trouble.

Many Minds Are Better Than One

As you look for potential crises, seek broad-based input. People's perspectives about risk differ, and some may see potential perils that others miss entirely. By talking with many people—project team members, employees in the operating units, corporate staff, customers, and suppliers—you may harvest some surprising information. For example, a distributor may tell you, "We've had a surprising number of your model 34-973 automobile tires returned by customers last month because of blowouts." That information should prompt you to look more closely. Tire blowouts are dangerous; they could result in customer injury and a costly product recall. The distributor's experience may be the tip of a dangerous but hidden problem for your company.

To make the most of the many insights available to you, people must feel free to speak their minds—that is, to speak openly about problems they see brewing. If whistle-blowers are routinely punished, or if higher management is dismissive of their warnings, employees will say nothing. For example, the field salespeople of one company complained among themselves that their bosses were spending too much time in their offices and on the golf course, and almost no time confronting competitive threats to the business. But no one said anything for fear of personal repercussions. The products of this company eventually lost market share, and the company itself was acquired by a competitor.

How open to warnings from employees is your organization? Are people who sound the alarm rewarded, ignored, or punished?

Use a Systematic Approach

The best way to complete a thorough risk audit is to approach it through operating units, departments, and work teams. Top management can provide important insights, but the people best equipped to detect crisis-producing situations are further down in the organization. These employees meet regularly to formulate plans and budgets, to assess competition and their own performance, and to identify opportunities for improvement. Risk identification should be on their list of things to do. Consider this example:

> *The managers of manufacturing, marketing, inventory control, and purchasing for BuildIt, a medium-sized manufacturer, are meeting to discuss work plans and production levels. They hold this meeting every few months. As a matter of policy, this group spends part of its time brainstorming risks to the business. Many of the risks it confronts are routine, such as potential injuries to production-line employees and major equipment breakdowns. These risks are addressed respectively through insurance, a rigorous plant safety program, and equipment redundancy, and so are not the main focus of the group's attention.*
>
> *What matters most to these managers are external risks over which they have little or no control. In the course of their brainstorming session, the marketing manager brings up the potential loss of a key customer. "Gizmo Products has accounted for almost 25 percent of our component sales for the past five years," says the marketing manager. "It has been a dependable customer." He then explains that Gizmo's purchasing manager, with whom he has enjoyed a good relationship, will be retiring later in the year: "The manager's replacement will be hired from the outside, so I'm not sure what to expect or where we'll stand with the Gizmo account. A new purchaser might want to review all major accounts, and that could result in an unfavorable change for us. With a new guy in there, we might stand a 50-50 chance of losing the account."*

*The assembled managers agree that the potential loss of the
Gizmo account should be listed as an important risk, one that would
adversely upset their plans and budgets. Could it lead to a financial
crisis for the company? "Twenty-five percent is a huge piece of our
business," says the manufacturing manager. "This is a risk we must
monitor closely."*

To be systematic in identifying potential crises, discussions like
that one should be conducted in all areas of the company, and at
every level. Don't leave it up to top management. Senior managers
aren't going to know about Henry, the frustrated and angry guy
doing data-entry work on the fourth floor. They won't know that
Henry's supervisor just passed him over for a promotion, giving the
job to Janice, whom Henry despises. Nor will they know that
Henry's wife just filed for divorce, demanding the house, custody of
the children, and two-thirds of Henry's take-home pay. No, top
management doesn't know anything about Henry, even though he's
a ticking time bomb who may explode without warning.

What are your company's ticking time bombs? Figure 1-1, "The
10 Worse Things That Could Happen List," contains a worksheet
that you and your colleagues can use to identify your key risks and
what you might do about them. You can download copies of this
same worksheet, and other useful tools, from the Harvard Business
Essentials series Web site: www.elearning.hbsp.org/businesstools.

Adopt the Mind of an Assassin

When people begin thinking about potential crises that might rock
their companies, they think primarily about crises they have already
experienced—or ones they've heard about in the news. Thinking
beyond the boundaries of personal experience is more difficult. But
that is where the real dangers often come from. Ian Mitroff and
Murat Alpaslan have suggested a novel technique for getting beyond
that boundary—adopting the role of internal assassin. They explain,
"We often ask . . . executives to imagine themselves to be internal as-
sassins or internal terrorists. That frees them to suspend their ration-

FIGURE 1-1

The 10 Worst Things That Could Happen List

Some managers find it helpful to create a list of the ten worst things that could happen at work and what they would do about those situations. Use this tool to record your own list, or have a team or work group develop a list.

Situation	What I/We Would Do About It
1.	
2.	
3.	
4.	
5.	
6.	
7.	
8.	
9.	
10.	

Source: Harvard ManageMentor® on Crisis Management.

ality and moral codes and allows them to use their intimate knowledge of the company's products, procedures, and systems to cook up ways to destroy it, either from the inside or the outside."[2]

Mitroff and Alpaslan cite the case of one medical insurance company whose executives formed into three teams of "terrorists." Each team was asked to devise schemes that individual employees, outsiders, and inside-outside swindlers could use to pilfer the company. "Much to everyone's surprise and embarrassment, all three teams came up with ingenious scams that the organization would not have been able to detect." The company was then told to assemble counterterror teams to find ways of thwarting the scams. This simulation pinpointed operational areas that were most vulnerable to fraud.

Tips for Identifying Potential Crises

Does your company have a systematic approach for identifying potential crises? If it doesn't, here are some practical suggestions:

- Make risk identification a regular component of business planning and evaluation. Once it becomes part of your management process, participants will become more conscious of the risks that could develop into full-blown crises. Some companies now have audit plans in place—these hold managers accountable for identifying threats on an ongoing basis. For threats such as fire and acts of violence, they conduct simulations with local authorities once or twice each year.

- Conduct risk identification at all levels, from top to bottom. Involve all relevant personnel.

- Look outside your organization as well as inside. That means including the thinking of customers, suppliers, industry analysts, and others.

- Think of all the ways you could create havoc for your company. What you can think of, others may do.

Can you think of ways to defraud your company and get away with it? Can you think of a way that you could physically harm your company's customers by tampering with its products? If you can, chances are that someone else can do the same.

Prioritizing Potential Crises

It wasn't too many years ago that the public first began to hear news reports about asteroids that might one day crash into our planet. A moderately large one, like the one that struck Siberia in 1908, would kill millions if it hit a populated region. A *really* big one could end civilization as we know it and push Homo sapiens into extinction. Talk about a potential crisis!

While a small number of scientists and some compulsive worriers have made the asteroid threat a top priority, the rest of us aren't losing any sleep over it. And the reason is simple: While the consequences of an asteroid strike could be catastrophic, the probability of an occurrence in our lifetimes and those of our immediate offspring is extremely small. Scientists believe that a Siberia-like event happens only once every thousand years or so. Few people are concerned about anything with these odds, even if its consequences would be huge. They have more immediate things to worry about: losing retirement money in the stock market, being hit by a speeding car, or facing a major illness. Each of those would result in a personal crisis, and each has some reasonable probability of actually happening. What keeps you awake at night?

Obviously, we are selective about the risks on which we concentrate our attention, and rightly so. Some risks are more worthy of our attention than are others—and we have only so much attention to spread around. In effect, we must allocate our attention to the greater risks. There is, however, substantial anecdotal evidence that people are not very good at dealing with risk. They will, for example, worry about being struck by lightning (an extremely low probability) but cross a busy city street (much higher probability of injury) without hesitation. For example, when the movie *Jaws* appeared in theaters in the 1970s, many people developed a visceral fear of going to ocean beaches. They imagined man-eating sharks lurking in the shallows, just waiting to attack! Many people actually cancelled beach vacations in favor of other activities. We know that the probability of being killed or injured by a shark in most areas is almost too small to calculate. The likelihood of an equally damaging auto accident, in contrast, is thousands of times greater, but that never stopped shark-fearing folk from driving on the nation's highways.

Unless we are thoughtful about the risks we face as business people, we may expend our attention on improbable risks while ignoring the risks that will really bite us. One method for avoiding this

mistake is to use a simple mathematical function called *expected value.*
In its simplest form, expected value is the anticipated outcome of an
event (E) times the probability of the event occurring (X), or

E(X) = expected value

That simple equation weights the anticipated outcome by the probability that it will happen.

Let's say that the cost of medical care, lost income, and personal
suffering from loss of a limb to a great white shark attack is $2 mil-
lion. The probability of such an attack is estimated as one in a million
(.0001 percent or .000001). For purposes of illustration, let's assume
that the cost of losing a limb due to an auto accident on the way to
work is the same. But the odds of it occurring are much higher: one
in one thousand (.1 percent or .001). Thus, the expected value of the
shark attack is: $2,000,000 × .000001 = $2.00. Not much to worry
about. In contrast, the expected value of the auto trip is $2,000, one
thousand times greater than the expected value of a shark attack.
This little calculation might convince someone to take that vacation
at the beach after all.

You can use this methodology to prioritize the attention you
should give to the many risks found through your crisis audit. That
audit will have identified dozens of risks to your company or unit. As
a first cut at prioritizing them, follow these steps:

Step 1: Make an estimate of the negative impact of each risk.
Express it in monetary form. For example, "The cost of a
one-month delay would be $25,000."

Step 2: Assign a probability to the risk (0 percent to 100
percent). For example, "The risk of a one-month delay is
40 percent (or .40)."

Step 3: Multiply the monetary impact times the probability.
Example: $25,000 x .40 = $10,000. That expected value is, in
effect, the dollar impact weighted by the probability of its
occurrence.

Step 4: Rank-order your audit list by expected value.

TABLE 1-1

BuildIt's Risks

Risk Description	Estimated Impact of Its Occurrence	Probability of Its Occurrence	Expected Value
Price of our components drops 10% across the board	$2 million in reduced gross operating earnings per year	35%	$700,000 in lost gross operating earnings per year
Loss of the Gizmo account	$4 million in lost revenues per year	50%	$2 million in lost revenues per year
Disruption of raw-materials supply due to a transportation strike	$300,000 in lost profits	15%	$45,000 in lost profits

A rank-order list will give you greater insights into the risks that you face. Table 1-1 indicates the expect value of three risks identified by managers at BuildIt, whom we met earlier in this chapter. As you can see, losing the Gizmo Products account would have the greatest probability-adjusted impact on the company, and it's here that BuildIt's managers and salespeople will want to concentrate their attention. If the company had many fixed costs, a revenue loss of that magnitude might push it into a financial crisis.

This mathematical approach may *not* be the best way to prioritize crisis potential in all cases. Here are two reasons why:

1. Assigning a low priority to a high-impact risk may simply be unacceptable to management—no matter how unlikely the occurrence—if an occurrence would spell disaster for the company.

2. Some risks are much easier and cheaper to neutralize than others. Thus, a risk with a $2 million expected value that's easy to avoid may be assigned a lower priority than another risk with only a $1 million expected value that's difficult to defend against.

So use expected value as a quantitative tool, and then apply qualitative evaluation to sort out your priorities.

You now understand the importance of auditing the risks that could throw your company into crisis and where to look for them. You also have some ideas for conducting that audit. The final section gave you a practical method for prioritizing your risks. You're now ready to move to the next idea: crisis avoidance.

Summing Up

- Crises have many sources, and these are often unique to a company's line of business.

- Accidents and natural events, health and environmental disasters, technical breakdowns, economic and market forces, and rogue employees are among the potential perils faced by organizations.

- As you audit potential crises, seek broad-based input. Many minds are better than a few.

- Conduct your organization's risk audit through its individual units. The people closest to its operations are best equipped to detect crisis-producing situations.

- One method for identifying potential crises is to put yourself in the role of an internal saboteur and ask, "What could I do to damage this company?"

- Some risks are more worthy of managerial attention than others.

- One way to prioritize crisis prevention efforts is to quantify risk in terms of their potential impact times and their probability of occurrence.

Avoiding the Avoidable

An Ounce of Prevention . . .

Key Topics Covered in This Chapter

- *How some managers and companies make crisis avoidance a routine practice*

- *Using a probability-based risk audit to determine the cost of risk avoidance*

- *The warning signs of impending crises*

- *Avoiding self-inflicted crises*

- *Using insurance to manage risk*

SCANNING THE SOURCES of risk to your business and conducting an audit of the things that could grow into crises are the first steps of crisis management. The next step, the subject of this chapter, is to determine which potential crises can be avoided. Good managers practice crisis avoidance every day. Consider these examples:

Helen is the financial manager of a medium-sized retail business. She foresees a possible cash shortage several months in the future, one that could create a crisis for the company. To avoid the shortage she takes a number of actions. First, she takes steps to assure that all receivables will be paid to her company on schedule. Second, working with the CEO, she puts a hold on all discretionary spending. Finally, she negotiates a $500,000 line of credit under good terms at her local bank. If the first two steps fail to stem the impending crisis, that last one will help the company weather the storm.

When informed that Jack, a key employee, has been interviewing with other companies, his boss tells himself, "If Jack leaves midway through the big project he's managing, we will be badly hurt." So the boss takes steps to identify an interim replacement, beginning within Jack's own unit. "Who could fill Jack's shoes tomorrow if need be?" the boss asks himself. "If no one is quite ready, what training or experience will our best internal candidates for the job need to make them ready?"

Fearful that the supply of a key component may be extremely limited six months in the future, Karl, the purchasing manager of an original equipment manufacturer, takes two crisis-avoiding steps. First, he builds a buffer stock of the component, enough to keep the production line running through many months of limited supply. Karl knows that excess component inventories are expensive, but he also knows that production shutdowns can be catastrophic. Second, he begins to build relationships with alternative suppliers. By giving these suppliers small orders of the component now, he opens up sources for larger orders in the future—when they might be critically needed.

Tom, a commercial real estate developer, has dealt with many building contractors over the years. Quality work has been a problem with only a few, but the cost of fixing even one poor job can be huge and can cause serious and costly schedule delays. Knowing from experience that many contractors cut corners to finish within budget and on time, Tom builds quality specifications into every contract; he then monitors compliance with those specifications on a regular basis. "If a contractor isn't doing the job right, I want to know about it early in the game," he says. "Left untended, little problems only grow bigger."

Each of those managers recognizes risks and has taken steps to avoid or mitigate them. Doing so is part of their jobs. Executives and managers in your company should do the same.

Crisis avoidance can be as mundane as the internal financial controls that prevent embezzlement or the squandering of corporate resources. Or it can be as complex as product design. Manufacturing companies are learning that they can avoid costly lawsuits, customer boycotts, and bad press by giving greater attention to product design. More specifically, they are learning how to design potential problems out of their products. Consider this example:

3M makes and sells hundreds of different film and adhesive products. All use chemicals of one kind or another in their manufacture. Back in the early 1970s, 3M was getting lots of pressure from newly established environmental protection agencies and from the public about the tons of pollutants it created each year. Seeing that the problem and 3M's image would do nothing but get worse, the company started a program to eliminate pollution at its source through product reformulation, modification of processes, equipment redesign, and the reuse of waste materials. That program, 3P (for Pollution Prevention Pays), has helped the company avoid regulatory

entanglements and has enhanced its public image. 3M estimates that
between 1975 and 2002, 3P has reduced its pollutant output by more
than 850,000 tons and saved the company almost $900 million.[1]

What potential crises could your unit or your company avoid through actions like 3M's? Manufacturers, chemical producers, and refineries are ideally positioned to use product and process design to avoid crises caused by the things they sell and by the processes they use to make those things.

Prepare a Systematic Program of Crisis Avoidance

If you have conducted a crisis audit, you are prepared for a systematic program of crisis avoidance. Just go down your list of potential sources of crises, and for each item involve the appropriate people in a discussion of this question: What could we do to avoid or neutralize this as a source of future problems? As you do this, you'll come to the inescapable conclusion that some risks are more costly to avoid than others. For example, the cost of avoiding a temporary electrical outage at your chain of five retail stores might be $5,000—the cost of five gasoline-powered electricity generators. On the other hand, the cost of avoiding a potential lawsuit for discrimination in hiring, firing, and employee advancement might be $100,000—spent on having a labor law expert review the company's employment procedures and practices, followed by training for all managers.

The following example indicates how a company or an operating unit might approach this problem. It follows the expected value approach introduced earlier—that is, the company estimates the financial impact of each potential crisis, the probability of each happening, and the expected value for each (financial impact times the probability). Here the company extends that approach by determining the cost of avoiding each potential crisis on its list:

Harold is director of information technology of a $300 million service
company. Because IT is so critical to the day-to-day functioning of the
company, senior management asked him to audit his operation and
identify every important source of information service disruption, to

estimate the probability of those disruptions, and to calculate their likely damages to the corporation.

Harold and his people complied with management's request. But they went a step further. They estimated the cost of avoiding each serious risk. "What we've accomplished so far is extremely valuable," said Harold, "but we have to recognize that avoiding some risks will be easy and avoiding others will be difficult and costly. So I'd like you to work together in estimating the cost of eliminating each of the risks on our list. Once we have that information, we can make better decisions about how we can best allocate our time and resources."

Harold's team dutifully complied with his request, submitting a report with the summary shown in table 2-1.

TABLE 2-1

Risk Summary

Source	Estimated Impact (per event)	Probability of Impact (per year)	Expected Value (estimated impact × probability)	Estimated Cost of Avoidance
Power outage (one full day or more)	$120,000/day	10%	$12,000 for one-day event; $36,000 for major event	$10,000 for standby generator
External network outage from storm or cut cable	$70,000	15%	$10,500	$60,000 for redundant network
Hard drive crashes in transaction and processing systems	$70,000	10%	$7,000	$90,000 for backup systems
Hacker attack	$120,000/day plus damage to customer relationships if data is stolen	8%	$9,600	$30,000 to upgrade current firewall and virus detection system
Physical disaster in the data center	$900,000 to replace systems; $500,000 in lost business, etc.	2%	$28,000	$300,000 for an off-site data center and $7,000 for an insurance premium on equipment

Using this summary, Harold's IT unit was able to comply with management's request and report the likely cost of avoiding IT-associated damages to the corporation. That put management in a much better position to make decisions, and it put Harold in a better position to negotiate for the improvements he needed to assure continuous service to the corporation and its customers. One of the first things he asked for—and received—was permission to spend $10,000 on a backup electric generator because the cost was less than the probability-adjusted cost of a power outage.

Heed the Signals of Impending Crisis

Not every crisis begins with a fire, a network outage, or other out-of-the-blue event. Many begin as small problems. Left unattended, they grow. If management fails to notice and neutralize them, they evolve into full-blown crises. Such signals should be considered here in the context of crisis avoidance.

Examples of creeping crises are many. One memorable case involved the venerable *New York Times,* a paper that has always prided itself on the quality of its reporting. The *Times* became the focus of a major and unflattering news story in the summer of 2003 when one of its young reporters, Jayson Blair, was accused of fabricating and plagiarizing news stories. That scandal left the *Times* newsroom in disarray and tarnished the paper's reputation for objective and credible reporting. Both its executive editor and managing editor were compelled to resign.

Sadly, the *Times*'s credibility crisis, like so many others that slam organizations, was completely avoidable. Several news editors had sent up warning flags about the quality of Blair's work, but management failed to heed them. Instead, it promoted him and gave him bigger stories to cover. Had it heeded these early warnings, the *Times* would have avoided a devastating incident.

What early warnings should you watch for in your business? There is no official list. Nevertheless, here is a handful of warning signs that a future crisis is brewing:

- **Too much success too soon.** A new sales representative is doing much, much better than anyone would reasonably anticipate. His manager has reason to be pleased, but the manager should also be alert to the possibility that his wunderkind sales rep is doing something illegal, unethical, or against company policy in bringing in those big sales. As one manager at a brokerage firm stated to the writer of this book, "I worry about newcomers who are doing too well."

- **An employee living beyond his means.** When a former Massachusetts treasury official with a $90,000 income bought a multimillion-dollar home outside of Boston, someone should have taken notice. That official—now in prison—was a member of an embezzlement ring that, when caught, embarrassed the state government and outraged Bay State taxpayers.

- **Inattention to details and standards.** We've all heard the expression, "The devil is in the details." Even small details can create a crisis if not attended to. Consider the sad case of ValuJet Flight 592. In May 1996, ground personnel loaded several oxygen-generating canisters into the cargo hold of this Atlanta-bound DC-9. Shortly after takeoff, a fire erupted in the hold, sending smoke through the passenger compartment and cockpit. Moments later, the aircraft plunged into the Florida Everglades, killing 110 passengers and crew members. ValuJet voluntarily suspended all of its flights pending an investigation and did not resume them for three months.[2] Federal investigators later said that many of the canisters were missing safety caps and a cargo manifest listed them as being empty when they were not. Attention to details and standards would have avoided this tragedy and the financial crisis that gripped ValuJet.

- **Board members who aren't doing their jobs.** Some board members forget that they work for the shareholders, not for the CEO. Others pick up hefty checks and stock options but pay little attention to corporate strategy or policies. Consider New York Stock Exchange (NYSE) board members, who raised

CEO Richard Grasso's annual pay to $146 million in 2003, creating a nationwide outcry and drawing the attention of exchange regulators. One board member lamely admitted to not being aware of Grasso's compensation. The NYSE case is not unique. Board members of Enron and WorldCom likewise failed to smell smoke that preceded the meltdown of those high-flying companies.

Remember that big crises often have small beginnings. So be alert to the warning signs of impending crises. Confront them quickly and decisively, and you will avoid big problems later.

Look Before You Leap

Some crises are self-inflicted, the result of managerial actions whose consequences were never systematically examined. Consider this hypothetical example:

> The board of Johnstone Machine Works has approved management's plan to close its 300-employee plant in the small town of Farmvale and transfer its operations to a newer, larger plant located in a city 300 miles away. Current employees will have first crack at jobs in the new plant, and many will have an early retirement option.
>
> Management has made a good business case for the move, which makes sense from a financial and operation perspective. But no serious thought has been given to the consequences for younger workers who cannot move and for the town of Farmvale itself. Johnstone is Farmvale's largest employer and taxpayer; a plant closure would devastate the town. What will this do to the company's reputation? How will this affect the reputation of Chairman and Founder Phil Johnstone, who has just begun his campaign for state governor?

In this example, no one has thought about the TV news images of angry workers and Farmvale citizens picketing outside Johnstone's offices. No one has anticipated media interviews with Farmvale storekeepers whose businesses will suffer with the plant closure.

Tips for Avoiding Trouble

Opportunities to protect your company and its employees from the perils of Mother Nature are limited. However, the company's behavior relative to employees, customers, suppliers, the government, and the media is controllable and can make the company less vulnerable to crisis. So observe these tips:

- Be a good corporate citizen in good times as well as bad. If you enjoy high standing with the public, you'll be supported rather than attacked during a crisis. Rightly or wrongly, Microsoft failed to develop a reputation as a corporate good guy. Many considered its business practices predatory, and the Internet became a popular forum for jokes about the flaws of its ubiquitous operating system. So when Microsoft was charged with antitrust violations, few rallied to its defense.

- Keep up collaborative relations with the media. If you are open, candid, and helpful to the press during normal times, the media will treat you more gently during periods of crisis. If you habitually ignore or act with hostility to the press, a sharp-penned reporter or commentator will likely skewer you the first time your company has trouble.

- Be highly ethical, trustworthy, and professional in your relations with the press, employees, customers, and suppliers. When a crisis hits, they will be sympathetic and inclined to help.

- Avoid technological breakdowns by keeping computers and other systems up-to-date, and attack problems quickly.

- Avert labor problems during crunch times by scheduling contract renewals and negotiations for times of the year when business is slow.

- Be alert to signals of impending crises. Don't ignore problems. Instead, confront and resolve them before they escalate into serious crises.

Continued

- Have a succession plan for all key positions. You can avoid some human-resource-related crises if you have qualified people capable of stepping into any potential vacancy.

- Don't cut corners when it comes to ethical and legal re-quirements. Doing so will eventually get you into trouble, causing a personal crisis for you and a financial or public relations crisis for your company.

Should the company proceed with its planned closure? Maybe. Per-haps it has no choice. But someone should have anticipated the pub-lic outcry that will follow. There may be a way to phase out the plant *and* avoid a public relations crisis.

Don't Forget About Insurance

Many of the damages associated with full-blown crises can be re-duced or eliminated through insurance. Insurance cannot help a company avoid crisis, but it can help it avoid some or all of the neg-ative financial consequences. In the example of Harold and the IT department, the company's hardware, software, and data center space could be covered under a corporatewide property insurance policy. Several lesser-known types of insurance are available to protect a business against important threats. These include life insurance on key employees and business interruption insurance.

Employee Life Insurance

The loss of key personnel due to disability or death is a constant peril, but one we seldom consider. Particularly in small, closely held companies, the value of the enterprise may be tied to the know-how, connections, or inventiveness of one or two individuals. Many businesses purchase so-called *key man* policies to protect themselves should these individuals die or become incapacitated.

> *Janice, now a 55-year-old estate-planning attorney, had built up a successful practice over the past two decades. Her firm had grown to four partners, seven associates, and six clerical employees. Nevertheless, Janice remained the rainmaker, the partner who brought in most of the firm's business. What would happen to the firm if something should happen to Janice? To hedge its risks, the firm took out a $1 million ten-year term insurance policy on Janice's life, naming itself as the beneficiary. If Janice died within the policy period, the firm would receive the $1 million death benefit, an amount deemed sufficient to allow it to survive and function until it could find a new leader.*

Other companies routinely take out policies on the lives of rank-and-file employees, with the company itself named as beneficiary. These policies, which typically carry death benefits equal to the annual incomes of the insured employees, are roughly the same amount the company would have to pay to recruit and train an adequate replacement for the deceased. This type of insurance makes sense from a business point of view, though it has the potential to upset some people. The revelation of this practice caused a minor stir back in 2001 when a national U.S. newspaper carried a full-blown story on it. Spouses of employees expressed shock that these companies would financially benefit from the death of their loved ones. The companies involved responded by making their case for the practice, explaining that they, and not the employees, were paying the premiums. The spouses, however, remained angry.

Business Interruption Insurance

Business interruption insurance is usually available under a larger property insurance policy and compensates the policy-owning company for lost income if it must vacate its premises due to disaster-related damages spelled out in the policy. For example, if the business has to shut down for three weeks because of a fire or flood, the insurance would offset a specified proportion of lost profits, as determined by the financial records of the policyholder. A policy may also cover monthly bills, such as telephone service, that continue even though business activities have come to a grinding halt. Like all insurance policies, the price of business interruption insurance premiums is related to the risks, as determined by the insurance underwriter, and to the size of the benefit paid in a claim.

Does your company use insurance to cover risks? Are its property and liability policies sufficient to guard against events that the company could not otherwise withstand? Be sure to get authoritative answers to those questions.

If you are a busy manager, you are probably thinking that this chapter has given you one more thing to do. You might be thinking, "In addition to putting out constant brush fires around here, I have to hire and fire, conduct performance appraisals on all my direct reports, produce a budget, and produce real results—not just reports. Now I'm supposed to conduct a thorough risk audit every year?"

You'd be justified in saying, "Forget about it" if the findings of your audit were not translated into appropriate actions. Either you—if you have the authority and resources—or senior management must (1) decide which risks to actively attempt to avoid, and (2) actually do something about them! Your assessment report should not go to the graveyard of corporate reports. The potential problems you've identified will not go away. And if any one of them should morph into a full-blown crisis, both you and senior management will regret that someone didn't do something to dodge the disaster.

Summing Up

- Some risks are potentially more dangerous or costly than others. Use a probability-adjusted risk assessment to determine which risks you can effectively neutralize through managerial action or insurance.

- Many crises begin as small problems. By heeding the signals of creeping crises, you can neutralize them before they grow dangerous and expensive.

- Some crises are self-inflicted. These can be avoided by thoughtful anticipation of the consequences of company policies and actions.

3

Contingency Planning

Preparing Today for
Tomorrow's Problems

Key Topics Covered in This Chapter

- *The five steps of contingency planning*

- *Addressing crises that cannot be anticipated through crisis management teams*

- *Using simulations to train crisis teams*

CHANCES ARE that you will be unable to reduce the potential impact or probability of some crises to acceptable levels. For example, a shop owner operating within a huge indoor shopping mall may do an exceptional job of fire prevention within her own store, but she cannot control the fire prevention practices of the other fifty shops that operate under the same roof. A major fire in any one of them could cause smoke and fire damage throughout the mall and interrupt business for weeks or months. For situations like these, crisis avoidance is not a viable approach; you must practice *contingency planning*.

Contingency planning involves organizing and making as many decisions as you can *before* a crisis occurs. Precrisis planning gives people the time they need to consider all options, think things through, discuss the merits of different reactions, and even test their preparedness to act. Each of those important tasks is much easier to do well in normal times, but difficult and stressful to do in the middle of a crisis.

As an example of contingency planning, consider how naval vessels deal with fire—a traditional threat to ships at sea. The captain and crew don't wait until an explosion ignites part of the ship and then hold a meeting to figure out what to do. Instead, fire control plans are developed and practiced before the ship ever leaves the dock. Every crew member—from officers to medics to designated fire control personnel—understands what to do and how to do it. Fire suppression equipment is sited throughout the ship.

We practice contingency planning all the time, usually without realizing it. A traveling salesman in the Canadian Rocky Mountains, for example, makes contingency plans for frigid winter road conditions. Knowing that he might be caught in a blizzard, or that his automobile might slip off the icy road and into a snowbank, he packs a shovel, a warm hat and gloves, some granola bars, and even a sleeping bag. And he makes sure that his flashlight and cell-phone batteries are charged.

Almost every organization practices some form of contingency planning. Cognizant of fire dangers, businesses appoint fire wardens for each floor of their office buildings and hold periodic fire drills. Major cities likewise develop plans for what they will do in the event of a biological warfare attack. They determine in advance how they will respond and where they will take victims for treatment. They even stockpile drugs and medical equipment so that they won't be caught short if and when these supplies are needed. The city of London has done the same, developing contingency plans for terrorist attacks in its underground transportation system.

Contingency plans are not designed to prevent crises. Instead, they are reactive and triggered by events. They can lessen the negative impacts of crises and return situations to normal more quickly.

You can develop effective contingency plans through the following steps:[1]

- **Step 1**: Organize a planning team.

- **Step 2**: Assess the scope of the problem.

- **Step 3**: Develop a plan.

- **Step 4**: Test the plan.

- **Step 5**: Keep the plan up-to-date.

Let's examine each of those steps, using a medium-sized, family-owned business as an example.

Step 1: Organize a Planning Team

Jack Elliot and his brother Bobby ran a successful company: Elliot Printing and Publishing. Their parents started the business in 1960 but had turned over most management responsibilities to the sons when they were old enough to handle the challenge. It was a good business, well-run and growing. The family shared the wealth via good pay and generous benefits with their unionized press operators, trimmers and packers, and shipping room personnel, and with nonunion salespeople, graphic artists, designers, and copywriters.

Everything was going well, and Jack thought of the business as one big, happy family. But when the union contract came up for review, Jack learned otherwise. Union workers, particularly the press operators, were very well paid, but they wanted much more, and they threatened to strike if their demands were not met. Jack had only six weeks to make a decision: Pay the price or risk a crippling strike.

Not one to waste time, Jack asked Bobby, who handled plant operations, to form a team to deal with the potential crisis. "I'll do my best to negotiate a contract acceptable to the union and to us," Jack told him. "But we should be prepared to weather a strike in the event that I fail. I'd like you to put together a team and work out a contingency plan for running this place without our union people. And I'd like you to start today."

Perhaps the biggest management lesson of the past dozen years is that teams can be extremely effective in handling complex, nonroutine jobs. Contingency planning is one of those jobs. A well-chosen team enriches the planning process with the skills and insights of many people. The team leader should enlist members with experience or special talents in each aspect of the potential crisis. This assures that nothing important will be overlooked.

Bobby Elliot sat down and began to make a list of the people he wanted on his team. The most affected areas would the unionized press room, the trimming and packing line, and the shipping room. Bobby managed each of those areas, but three nonunion supervisors were closest to the action. They belonged on the team. So did the sales manager, since customers would be concerned about the ability of Elliot Printing and Publishing to deliver their orders during a strikebound period.

Bobby's team expanded as he and others identified areas of concern. For example, Herb Schwartz, the company's financial officer, was added to the team to deal with the financial aspects of the potential strike. So too was the company's semiretired founder, William Elliot. The senior Elliot was highly articulate and had deep connections in the community and the local media. He agreed to act as public spokesperson for the company.

Step 2: Assess the Scope of the Problem

Once a team is formed, it must assess the scope of the problem. That means thinking of all the things that could go wrong and might need tending if the crisis were to occur. Here are a few tips for assessing problem scope:

- Many minds are better than one.

- Use informal brainstorming sessions to identify all important issues.

- Appoint one team member to capture people's ideas by recording them on a flipchart or whiteboard. Combine related ideas under common headings (e.g., answering customer questions and fielding reporters' questions would fall under the "Communications" heading).

- Once the team has assessed the problems, share your findings widely. Other employees may know of things you've overlooked.

Bobby's team met at the family lake home for its brainstorming session. It was a beautiful day, and the surrounding woods were bursting with autumn colors. After a half-hour hike, they got down to work.

The team decided to attack the problem by identifying fronts on which a strike would produce serious problems: meeting production schedules, customer relations, community relations, mental and physical stress on nonstriking employees, booking new sales, and physical security. Later, the team member from the shipping room added another: "Let's not forget that union drivers who work for our paper suppliers might refuse to cross the picket line. Unless we find a way to move supplies in and finished orders out, we'll be in big trouble." His concern was added to the list.

By the end of the day, the team had compiled a large set of things that could jeopardize continued operation of the company during a strike. Bobby Elliot then gave each team member an action assignment: "I want you all to meet with the nonunion people in your respective units. Show them the list, and ask them to identify anything we've missed. Also, gather their ideas for combating these problems. I'll run the list by Jack, human resources, and our lawyer. We'll reconvene next Tuesday."

Step 3: Develop a Plan

Once all of the ideas about what could go wrong have been captured and distilled into an actionable set of targets, it's time to develop a plan for addressing each (or as many as you have the resources to handle). The goal should be to develop and prepare for a set of actions that would neutralize or contain every significant aspect of a potential crisis. Again, this should be done by the team, with the advice and concurrence of other managers and employees.

Let's return to the Elliot company case to see how its contingency team planned for two key threats.

As a first step, the Elliot team decided to plan for two of its most pressing threats: a stalled production line and getting materials through a picket line of striking workers. Of those, the first posed the greatest challenge.

The heart of Elliot Printing and Publishing's operation was its three computer-controlled, state-of-the-art printing presses. Union employees—who threatened to walk out—operated those presses. How could the company keep the presses rolling without them? Fortunately, Bobby Elliot and the production supervisor knew the ins and outs of the equipment as well as any of the company's six press operators. "They really aren't that complicated," the supervisor told the team. "With a few weeks of hands-on training and supervision, any of our

Don't Forget Communications

Every contingency plan should include a communication plan—one capable of speaking to stakeholders. Decide who should know about the crisis, both inside and outside the organization. Then develop a plan so that those individuals will be informed as needed. A communication plan can be as simple as an emergency contact list, or it can take the more complex form of a communication tree that designates the flow of messages. (For a sample emergency contact list and the information it should contain, see the "Emergency Contact List" in appendix A.)

Effective internal communication bolsters employee morale and puts a damper on the energy-sapping rumors that go hand-in-hand with every serious crisis. Effective external communication likewise puts a lid on rumors and speculation and lets the public know that management is aware of the problem, takes it seriously, and is working toward a solution.

Here are a few things to remember with respect to communications:

- Communicate a small number of carefully chosen messages that correctly represent the problem and the company's response. Too many messages will confuse your audience.

- Have one official—not necessarily the CEO—present the big picture. Let other spokespersons address technical issues; they'll know more about those issues and will have greater credibility.

- Don't attempt to minimize the situation. Don't say, "Yes, our tanker has spilled a half-million barrels of oil near the beaches of Alicante, but compared to the *Exxon Valdez* incident, it's a small thing.

- Don't blame the victims. Firestone didn't help itself when it initially blamed poor customer maintenance for its tire failures.

Continued

In contrast, an Oregon-based manufacturer of school buses accepted responsibility for a problem with defective brakes and conveyed its aggressive plan for fixing them.

- Communicate all the bad news at once. It's better to be pummeled one time than it is to take a beating every time you announce yet another negative piece of information.

- Don't lie or speculate. If you're proved wrong on either score, your credibility will suffer.

- Never forget about your employees. Develop a plan to keep them fully informed. Speak to them often.

Adapted with permission from Harvard Business School Publishing, "How to Keep a Crisis from Happening," *Harvard Management Update*, December 2000, 6.

other employees could operate these machines." And Bobby found several nonunion employees who were willing to give it a try. Bobby and the supervisor then contacted the equipment manufacturer to arrange for training services, to begin the following week.

Getting materials through a union picket line represented another serious challenge, but one for which there was a solution. Bobby recruited two graphic designers to act as truck drivers if needed during the course of a strike. He arranged for these individuals to attend a three-day driving course, which would certify and license them as commercial vehicle operators.

Each of these aspects of the strike contingency plan was passed by Herb, the financial officer, and described to the company's attorney for comments and suggestions.

Step 4: Test the Plan

Never assume that the contingency plans you've worked out on paper will actually work. Always test them under simulated conditions. That's what we do when we have fire drills in our offices and schools. That's what the armed forces do when they introduce new equipment or tactics. And that's what the Elliot crisis team did.

> *William Elliot, founder of the company, stepped up to the podium. Looking out at his audience, he began his speech. It was brief and to the point, explained the situation candidly, and articulated the company's point of view: "We are now in the second day of a strike by Printers Local #31," he began. "As you probably know, this strike is the result of a failure by Elliot Printing and Publishing and the union to reach agreement on a new contract. The primary sticking point is hourly pay."*
>
> *He went on to describe the offer his company had put on the table and his view that the offer was generous: "Over the years, our employees have enjoyed pay raises as high or higher than the rising cost of living. This latest offer follows that pattern. At the same time, many key costs of running our business—from paper to workers' compensation insurance to health care benefits—have risen dramatically. These rising costs make it extremely difficult to make our current pay offer more generous. Also, we are faced with growing competition from nonunion printers, who pay an average of 23 percent less than the offer we have made to our union employees."*
>
> *In the next brief statements, the elder Elliot described how management and nonunion personnel were prepared to continue operations at near-normal levels, and he assured the company's customers that all current and new orders would be filled on time. He finished by expressing his hope that the impasse would be quickly settled and that union personnel would be back to work.*
>
> *Mr. Elliot's audience for this speech was not a gaggle of local new reporters but Jack, Herb, and a half-dozen other employees. This was strictly a test run of a presentation they planned to make if the threatened strike became a reality. It would be critiqued and improved as needed. Meanwhile, a training representative from the printing press vendor had been holding evening classes for those employees designated to take over press operations in the event of a strike. All planned to come in on Saturday morning to apply their learning to a simulated print job. These individuals would receive additional pay for weekend work.*

Next week Jack and a hired labor specialist would work out the details of their plan to negotiate with the union.

The kind of contingency plan testing undertaken by the Elliots and their employees demonstrates the best way to discover weaknesses and opportunities for improvement. It is also a very good way to build confidence in the organization's ability to control and vanquish a looming crisis.

Step 5: Keep the Plan Up-to-Date

If your company has a contingency plan for fire emergencies, it has probably assigned one or more fire marshals to each floor and trained those individuals in how to respond. Individual employees have likewise been trained in how to exit the building quickly and safely.

Plans, however, cannot be set and forgotten. Things change. In the case of a fire plan, new floor marshals have to be recruited as others retire or leave the company. New employees must be given fire instructions. Home phone numbers change often and must be updated periodically. Periodic fire drills must be held to reinforce people's understanding of emergency procedures. Yes, updating is necessary but almost always easier to do than developing a contingency plan from scratch.

Six weeks after Jack Elliot sounded the alarm about a potential strike, the crisis management team headed by Bobby Elliot had developed and tested its contingency plans. Management judged the company ready to keep its presses rolling for a sustained period without its union workers. Bobby had even formed a rapid-reaction team that was ready to pounce on unanticipated adverse developments. This state of preparedness gave Jack enormous confidence when he went off to negotiate the new union contract.

In the end, labor and management succeeded in hammering out a mutually agreeable three-year deal. There was no strike. Bobby's team celebrated the good news later that week with a barbecue at the Elliot family lake house. Jack thanked its members for putting him in a strong negotiating position: "If you hadn't done what you did, the company would have faced two bad alternatives: pay up or temporarily shut the plant." The company founder seconded Jack's comment, adding one of his own.

"I've been in this business for more than forty years now," William Elliot reminded them, "and I can tell you that dangers like the one you've just avoided are always out there. This labor contract, for example, will expire in three years. Three years go by very quickly, especially when you're my age. My advice to you is this: Keep your team together. As we get new equipment, learn to use it. Think things through, and make routine decisions in advance, when everyone has a cool head and is not driven by the panic of the moment. Keep your eye on potential crises, and be ready to meet them head-on."

Are You Ready?

If you've developed a crisis audit, take a look at it today. Chances are that it lists many risks capable of severely damaging your company or your particular unit. Have you developed contingency plans for the most important of those risks? If you haven't, start today, following the five steps described in this chapter. Once you've finished, the company should have a solid contingency plan for every key threat it faces: a fire, a natural disaster, an act of violence, a strike, and so forth.

Where to Start

Don't know where to start? Then start with something simple. If your company operates in an area subject to winter blizzards, begin there. Determine under what circumstances your offices or plants should be closed. What weather or driving conditions should trigger a decision to close? (One school principal used this rule of thumb: He would drive to the school two hours before the normal opening time; if the snow was so deep that he could not get to the school and park in the lot, he would declare an official snow day.) Then determine who should make the decision. In many cases this is the head of human resources.

There should also be a clear plan for passing the word to employees. For example, the plan might call for the head of HR to call the CEO and to then call each of the CEO's direct reports. Those individuals would be responsible for calling their direct reports. And so it would go down the chain of command until every employee was informed. Alternatively, the message might be placed on a special phone line that any employee could call. A weather emergency plan should also determine when and how employees will be recalled to work.

These chores are better settled *before* rather than during a real emergency. Once you've developed and tested a workable plan for something this simple, move on to more challenging potential crises.

Planning for the Crisis You Cannot Anticipate

Everything said so far about identifying potential crises assumes a certain clairvoyance, and that is not realistic. We cannot anticipate every threat, yet it's often these unforeseen threats that do the greatest damage. For instance, British defenders of Singapore in 1941 had fortified their citadel with concrete bunkers and a formidable array of artillery batteries, most facing seaward. Any force approaching from the sea would have been annihilated. And how else could one approach Singapore? The city's backdoor was defended by the impenetrable jungle of the Malay Peninsula, which is exactly where the Japanese army chose to launch its attack. The possibility of an attack from that direction was not anticipated, and so there was no plan.

Could Kodak, maker of photography film, have ever anticipated that the biggest threat to its business would be from an electronics company? Clearly not. It had focused its attention and competitive plans on rival film producers, Fuji in particular. Yet when Sony, a leading consumer electronics producer, introduced the first commercial digital camera, it opened a backdoor to Kodak's defenses.

Could Tokyo authorities have anticipated that anyone would release a deadly gas in the city's subway system? Today, in the aftermath of many terror attacks around the world, we can imagine such a senseless act. But in 1995, the year in which the Aum Shinrikyo cult perpetrated the attack, the idea that anyone would gas defenseless people was beyond comprehension. And so there was no plan for dealing with such an emergency.

How can we plan for threats we cannot anticipate? Is it even possible?

The five-step approach offered in this chapter will not help you prepare for the threats you cannot envision. How could they? But that is no excuse for defeatism or passivity. At a minimum, you can be prepared to act—whatever the crisis.

You can ready yourself and your company by establishing a crisis management team of highly flexible and decisive individuals with organizational authority. This team should have clear lines of communication to the police, fire department, emergency medical personnel, and stakeholders inside and outside the company. In a large corporation, that team should include the chief operating officer, corporate counsel, and the heads of investor relations, communications or public relations, and human resources. The chief executive and chief financial officers should be *ex officio* team members. This team should be small enough to make decisions rapidly and communicate without impediment. At the same time it must be large enough to tap all the source of expertise needed to respond to a crisis situation. This team needs one other feature: the power to act. A crisis team without action power is useless.

Training Simulations

Appointing people to a crisis team in advance of real trouble is a good first step toward being ready to act in any crisis situation, but people must learn to work together and respond quickly. This learning only comes from doing, which is why many crisis experts recommend that crisis management teams hone their skills with simulations. The military, police, fire departments, airline pilots, and emergency medical personnel all use simulations to perfect their skills and to prepare themselves for unusual situations. Crisis management teams can and should do the same.

Here are just a few examples of simulations that a crisis team might use as practice:

- Toxins have been found in the company's offices. Personnel must be evacuated quickly and for an undetermined period of time. The proper authorities must be alerted.

- The company has just received an e-mail: "We have your East Asian division manager and his family. Give us $5 million, or their blood will be on your hands."

- The union steward has been fired for chronic tardiness, and the union local is threatening a walkout if she is not immediately reinstated.

- A discharged employee returns to confront his supervisor. He is heavily armed and threatening to shoot the supervisor and two other hostage employees.

What Would You Do?

Picture yourself working in your office. You've just returned from a lunch meeting with a customer. It has been a normal and uneventful day.

Suddenly, you hear people screaming. Someone shouts, "He has a gun!" People are running in a panic past your open door. You go to the door and glance cautiously up and down the corridor. David Johnson is peering over the top of his cubicle. Most of the other employees are pushing and shoving to get through the doorway to the rear stairwell. "I think he's gone upstairs," David yells to you as he too races toward the stairwell.

You begin to feel the same panic that has infected everyone else. Adrenaline courses through your system. "Who's out there?" you wonder. "Will he come back this way? Is anyone hurt?"

What would your emotions be in such a moment? As the one person left on the floor, what would you do? Imagined scenarios like these can help you prepare for the real thing.

What would your company do? By working on these simulated situations, the crisis team will learn several things: how to make decisions under time pressures, whom they can turn to for different types of assistance and information, what is legal and what is not, and so forth. These simulations can be both exciting and highly productive. They can prepare your team to act rapidly and decisively, no matter what the crisis happens to be.

How One Company Plans and Prepares for Crises

Few industries are as exposed to crises and catastrophes as the airline industry. Considering the billions of passenger miles flown yearly by the world's major airlines, it's a wonder that incidents are so few. Some events—such as strikes—are nonlethal. Others have the potential of causing great loss of life. A plane crashes on takeoff. Another disappears somewhere over the Atlantic. Armed hijackers divert another flight, holding passengers and crew members hostage. In the worst of all imaginable scenarios, terrorist commandeered three flights and crashed them into office buildings in New York City and Washington, DC, compounding the human and material damage.

The major airlines have learned the hard way that crises can strike anytime, anywhere, and entirely without warning. Consequently, they have been among the leaders in crisis planning and preparedness. United Airlines provides a good example.

United's Operations Control Center is located in Elk Grove Village, IL, not far from Chicago's O'Hare Airport. This nerve center tracks weather, takeoffs and landings, passenger information, flight delays, and the availability of aircraft and crews within United's worldwide system. It manages supply and demand for flights and works to minimize delays and cancellations due to mechanical problems and weather. These controls are a necessary part of operating a large, modern airline. More is needed, however, to handle the crises to which United and every other air carrier are exposed every day.

Nestled in the same complex is United's crisis management gathering place—the Special Operations Center. This is where United's crisis team meets and acts when a crisis strikes. As described by author and crisis consultant Steven Fink, permanent members of the team include managers of public relations, flight operations, flight safety, corporate security, in-flight personnel, marketing and customer service, medical services, and the Federal Bureau of Investigation. United's CEO and board chairman are *ad hoc* members. Others are enlisted as needed.[2] The center is supported by state-of-the-art information and communications technologies. An inch-thick folder that details precisely what United's people in the field should do to handle a crisis is available and constantly updated. When a crisis strikes, United is ready.

How prepared is your company to face a crisis—either predictable or unimagined? Do you have a contingency plan in place? Is there a crisis team at the ready? If you answer no to any of those questions, it's time to get your act together. And the sooner the better.

Summing Up

- The first step of contingency planning is to organize a planning team that brings together the skills, experience, and insights of many people.

- The planning team should assess the scope of potential problems—that is, all the things that could go wrong.

- Develop a contingency plan that will neutralize or contain every significant aspect of a potential crisis. Communications should be part of the plan.

- Never assume that your contingency plans will actually work. Always test them under real or simulated conditions.

- Keep all contingency plans up-to-date.

- If you don't know where to start with contingency planning, start with simple contingencies, such as floods or fires.

- Contingency planning does not work for crises that cannot be anticipated. The best remedy in these cases is a crisis management team of people who are flexible, decisive, and have authority to act.

4

Crisis Recognition

Where There's Smoke,
There's Fire

Key Topics Covered in This Chapter

- *Seven indications that crises are taking shape*

- *Why warning signs are often unheeded*

- *Practical tips for crisis recognition*

HAVING A CRISIS management team at the ready and armed with contingency plans is always prudent. If a crisis appears, the team will be prepared to address it before too much damage is done. All the team needs is a signal of trouble, and it's ready to pounce!

But what signals a crisis? How will you know that it's time to act?

Some crises are self-evident. Firefighters are pumping water through the windows of your building as you pull into the parking lot. The morning newspaper has a picture of your CEO on the front page—in handcuffs. Unfortunately, not every crisis announces itself that emphatically. Many begin as small embers that grow hotter, eventually igniting everything around them. When crises start small, people may fail to recognize what is going on under their noses. By the time they notice what is happening, the crisis has grown to the point that it is dangerous and difficult to contain.

This chapter addresses the problem of crisis recognition and what you can do to make sure that warning signals are recognized and heeded in a timely way.

Different Warning Signals

If yours is a business organization, the warning signals of crisis can take many forms. Look for them among the traditional sources of crisis (natural disasters, technology breakdowns, etc.) listed earlier. Also be alert to the following.

A Technical Discontinuity

A technical discontinuity is an innovation that represents a major and profound departure from the entrenched technology of the day. The development of the transistor at Bell Labs in the 1950s was a technical discontinuity, one that earned its innovators a Nobel Prize. Development of the transistor also signaled the end of an era for the vacuum-tube technology that dominated the electronics industry at the time. It was a new wave. Companies that failed to heed the signal and get on the new wave experienced diminishing fortunes in the years ahead. Before long, vacuum tubes were used in only a few specialized applications, and the fortunes of the leading tube makers faded.

Public Resistance to an Innovation

When it comes to food products, the public is wary of anything that appears altered or adulterated. This is particularly true in Europe where resistance to U.S. meat products raised with growth hormones has been strong and has a long history. That signal did not seem to register with Monsanto, which continued to invest heavily in genetically altered crops. Today, the introduction of those crops is being resisted by farmers, environmentalists, consumer groups, and regulators in Europe, Canada, and Asia.

Warnings from Building, Safety, or Health Inspectors

A pattern of minor carelessness is often a signal that something very bad is bound to happen. For example, the owners of a nightclub on Chicago's South Side had been warned more than once about fire safety violations by building inspectors. These were signals that dangerous if not deadly consequences could follow. But the owners paid little heed. One Saturday night, a fight erupted in the club, and security guards responded with blasts of pepper spray. The resulting crowd panic resulted in more than twenty deaths due to trampling and suffocation. This disaster would have been avoided had the owners heeded the signals given to them by the inspectors.

Does you company have a pattern of building, health, or safety warnings? If it does, it may be in line for a serious mishap and crisis.

Persistent Rumors and Suspicions

Most of the rumors that get passed around an organization are nothing more than idle chatter and quickly dissipate. But others persist, often because they contain a kernel of truth—another warning sign that something bad is in the works. Consider the following example:

> *Not many years ago, the CEO of a major corporation was alerted that the president of one of its subsidiaries—a film company—was suspected of embezzling money and forging checks. The CEO refused to believe that this individual would ever commit such crimes and so ignored what he had heard. But the issue didn't go away. Eventually, what many had suspected was revealed to be true. By the time the CEO decided to fire the mischievous president, the charming thief had lined up board members on his side. The board insisted on keeping him. The situation worsened, and news reports tarnished the name of the film company, the corporation, and everyone involved—including the CEO. It was an ugly, painful situation, and one that could have been avoided had it been recognized as a potential crisis and dealt with promptly.*

Persistent Customer Complaints

The U.S. Catholic Church had for years received complaints from parishioners concerning pedophile priests. This shameful and criminal behavior was not new within the Church. It was not something that its leaders cared to discuss publicly, nor did they confront it within their own ranks. In many instances their solution was to hush up accusations and reassign errant clerics to other parishes, where some created new mischief. The warning signs of crisis were all there.

The pedophile problem eventually blew up into a national scandal that cost the Church millions and is likely to tarnish its reputation for a generation or more. Ironically, similar unheeded complaints by

Church "customers" back in the fifteen and sixteenth centuries led to another major crisis. Back then, the complaints had to do with the sale of indulgences (i.e., remission of afterlife punishment for sins), the moral laxity of the clergy, and the excessive wealth of the Church. These unheeded complaints eventually erupted into the Protestant Reformation that has divided Christendom ever since.

Are your customers telling you something about dangerous conditions associated with your products or about questionable practices by your company's sales representatives? If they are, they may be signaling an impending crisis.

Lax Management Standards

Any company that allows managers to play fast and loose with regulatory rules in hiring, sales practices, supervisory practices, and so forth sends a signal that big trouble may be just down the road. One nationwide restaurant chain in the United States, for example, was rife with problems of illegal discrimination against minority employees and customers in some of its locations. These problems were common knowledge inside the company, yet the leadership did nothing about them. Predictably, the company was slapped with civil rights violations, public embarrassment, and discrimination lawsuits that cost millions.

Pleas from Lower-Ranking Employees

In many cases, employees try to alert management of problems or dangers, but these issues fail to get a proper hearing. Prior to the explosion of the U.S. space shuttle *Challenger* in 1987, for example, the management of a key contractor received a number of urgent memos begging attention to what some people saw as a dangerous engineering problem, one that might destroy the shuttle. Those memos never registered with controllers of the program. Disaster followed.

More recently, the "market-timing" scandal that threw Boston-based Putnam Investments, a major mutual fund company, into both

regulatory and business crises could have been avoided if management had heeded the warnings of one of its employees. As described
in the *Wall Street Journal*:

> *Ignoring bad news doesn't make it go away, it causes spiraling
> problems. Executives at Putnam Investments, now under investigation
> for mutual-fund trading abuses, and Securities and Exchange Commis-
> sion officials tripped on that lesson.*
>
> *One of Putnam's call-center employees, Peter Scannell, spent close
> to two years trying to warn several of his supervisors about heavy "mar-
> ket timing" trades aimed at reaping short-term profit. The trades, while
> legal, hurt long-term investors and thus violated internal guidelines at
> mutual-fund companies. But Putnam managers ignored his warnings,
> he says. So did [Securities and Exchange Commission] officials in
> Boston, whose help he sought this past spring. He finally got a hearing
> in September [2003] from state regulators in Massachusetts, who used
> his information to launch an investigation of Putnam, one of many
> mutual-fund companies now being investigated.[1]*

Putnam paid dearly for its failure to heed this employee's warnings. It agreed to calculate and compensate fund shareholders for
damages going back to 1998. Worse, the market-timing scandal in-
duced a number of its largest pension fund clients—investors with
multibillion-dollar accounts—to shift their assets elsewhere. By one
estimate, some $13.2 billion was pulled out of Putnam in November
2003 alone. And since fund managers are paid a percentage of assets
under management, the scandal greatly diminished Putnam's future
earnings.[2]

The warning signs cited in this section are not the only harbin-
gers of future crisis. For a larger list and a handy tool for thinking
through them, see the "30 Warning Signs of Potential Trouble" checklist in appendix A.

Why Warnings Are Often Unheeded

It's clear in retrospect that each of the disasters described so far—and
many like them—could have been avoided or mitigated had some-

one with the authority to act heeded their warning signals. This begs the question, Why do signals of impending crisis fail to get through or register? Possible explanations include underestimating the problem, hubris, and failing to "connect the dots."

Underestimating the Problem

Do you remember the huge flap in 1994 over Intel's Pentium chip? That chip did everything well except for one type of mathematical calculation, a problem that hardly anyone would notice or care about. One who noticed *and* cared was a college professor, who contacted the company about the problem. As told by Norm Augustine: "So confident was the company in its product that it reportedly gave the professor a polite brush-off. Turning to the Internet to see if others could confirm the problem he had encountered, [the professor] triggered an avalanche of some 10,000 messages."[3] The story soon hit the media, spawning dozens of e-mail jokes and lots of bad press, all at Intel's expense.

Here, what seemed like a small problem to Intel officials was perceived differently by many customers of the company, who were as offended by Intel's attitude as by the chip defect. This was a clear case of underestimating a problem.

Hubris

Hubris—or excessive pride—is particularly deadly for successful organizations. It encourages self-satisfaction and an air of invulnerability, blinding leaders to signs of impending trouble. As just one example of organizational hubris, consider how General Motors executives failed to heed important warnings that the value of their products in the eyes of customers was being eclipsed by products made by foreign rivals.

When J.D. Power and Associates published its initial survey of auto industry quality and customer satisfaction back in the early 1980s, Japanese vehicles took all the top rankings. The industry's biggest producer, U.S.-based General Motors (GM), found itself on the outside looking in. Data from other sources, including GM's own documented quality problems with its X-car and J-car plat-forms, only confirmed J.D. Power's assessment. Managers of GM's corporate quality and reliability (Q&R) department took these dis-turbing findings seriously, but corporate leaders did not; they were firm in their conviction that GM set the standard against which all other automakers were measured. After all, theirs was the biggest, strongest automaker in the world.

Sensing the rising importance of quality standards, corporate Q&R undertook a benchmarking study involving eleven companies known for the quality of their products. GM did not look good in the study's findings. When presented to senior management in late 1984, those findings received a chilly reception and little attention.[4]

We can only speculate on why GM's leadership failed to heed clear warning signals of trouble from both outside and inside. Was it hubris? Were the people at the top just too focused on other issues to listen? Whatever the reason, the failure of the Detroit giant to get on the quality bandwagon quickly provided Asian competitors like Toyota and Nissan with opportunities to expand market share at GM's ex-pense. And once that share was lost, it was never recovered, despite more than twenty years of trying.

Failing to Connect the Dots

In the wake of the 9/11 terrorist attack in the United States, the Federal Bureau of Investigation (FBI) was criticized for failing to "connect the dots"—that is, for failing to connect separate pieces of intelligence into a coherent picture of the attackers' plan. If that crit-icism was true (and it remains to be proved), that intelligence failure was similar to the one that led to the country's earlier military disas-ter at Pearl Harbor on December 7, 1941. In that case, a number of intelligence and military reports and U.S. State Department mes-sages provided bits and pieces of information that, had they been brought together, would have identified the where, when, and how of Japan's aerial attack on the strategic Pacific base. But that did not happen. The navy had some information, the army had others, and the State Department had still others. These separate organizations, however, were not structured to share what they knew. The information was kept in separate pockets and never came together to form a coherent picture of the planned attack. Large corporate organizations often suffer from the same affliction. Useful data gathered by different functions does not always come together; making it difficult for decision makers to connect the dots and foresee a developing crisis.

Solutions

Underestimating problems, managerial hubris, and failing to connect the dots—those are timeless aspects of human behavior that prevent people from recognizing crises in the making. We see them repeated over and over in every century and in every part of the world. The question is, What can be done about them, and what can be done to make crisis recognition more likely?

To recognize a crisis before it happens or in its early stages you need organizational mechanisms for the following:

- Identifying the warning signs of crisis

- Sounding the alarm to people with the authority to act

Consider these three recommendations:

1. **Empower rank–and–file employees.** Don't expect senior management to do the job. Senior management is so preoccupied with keeping the company running that it is often in the worst position to recognize some impending crises. The warning signs of future crises are often most observable by rank-and-file employees, the people on the front lines of the business: field sales and service personnel, safety supervisors, quality inspectors, accountants, and technical professionals. These people must be empowered and encouraged to speak up when they see something that is terribly wrong. This will not happen when employees are encouraged to "shut up and follow orders." Nor will it happen in a work place dominated by fear.

2. **Make sure that someone is alert to their warnings.** A tree falling in the forest makes a sound *only* when there are ears to hear it. So instruct supervisors and managers to act as listening posts. Make it clear that attention to this matter is one of their many responsibilities. Doing so is particularly important when a company's leaders and managers are the problem. As Norm Augustine wisely noted, "Asking people who were responsible for preventing a problem whether or not there is a problem is like delivering lettuce by rabbit."[5]

Mediocre or inept supervisors and managers may be ineffective as listening posts. If you needed one more excuse for getting rid of C-level managers and executives, this is it. Replace them with people who (1) are alert to potential problems and (2) listen to the employees who report to them.

3. **Form a core crisis team.** Per an earlier recommendation, establish a core crisis team—a small group of people with complementary skills trained to develop contingency plans and to respond to crises as they develop. If managers aren't listening, empowered employees should be able to bring their warnings of impending crises to this team. A large organization needs a point, an intelligence center, where the bits and pieces of internal and external danger signs come together—and where the dots can be connected. Vincent Barabba and Harvard Professor Gerald Zaltman suggested such a place in their 1991 book, *Hearing the Voice of the Market.*[6] Although their concern was strictly about market information and market signals, Barabba and Zaltman's suggestion for an "inquiry center" is equally valid for crisis-related information. Such a center would be a physical unit within which a small staff with cross-functional training could accumulate and examine data. Only a large organization can afford such a unit. For smaller companies, a standing crisis management team can serve the same function with less cost.

How prepared is your company to recognize the warning signs of crisis? If a potential crisis arrived on its doorstep today, would any-

Tips for Recognizing Impending Crises

Many managers—like other people—are reluctant to face unpleasant situations. They either do not believe the bad news or would rather not deal with it. Not every problem is a crisis in the making; managers would dissipate every measure of their energy if they treated problems as such. So how can they recognize a crisis when they see it? Here are a few suggestions.

- Pay attention when your instincts tell you that there's something wrong.

- Confront disturbing facts as you find them. Don't ignore them, rationalize them, or minimize their importance. Instead, investigate.

- Consider the consequences if disturbing facts are found to be true (i.e., financial losses, physical injury, company reputation, etc.).

- Ask questions: Is this the tip of a big, dangerous iceberg? What are the dimensions of the problem right now? Could they grow larger and more dangerous?

- Seek the counsel of others, particularly those close to the situation.

- Let your values guide you. What is important? What is the right thing to do? For example, if a subcontractor is illegally disposing of toxic waste from your company, harming the environment, and possibly endangering lives, and you suspect the company is turning a blind eye to it, do what your values urge you to do: Confront the situation. Don't ignore it.

one notice? Who would sound the alarm? Would people with authority respond? To answer those important questions, examine your company in terms of the three barriers to crisis recognition just described: a tendency to underestimate problems, hubris, and having no way of connecting the dots. Get those things right, and you'll have a much better chance of catching a potential crisis before it hits, or before it has time to develop into a major problem.

Summing Up

- Many crises originate in a technical discontinuity or public resistance to a particular innovation in which a company is deeply invested.

- Building, safety, and health inspectors often sound an early warning of disaster.

- Listen carefully to persistent customer complaints. They often reveal the tip of largely hidden systemic problems.

- Lax standards with respect to hiring, supervisory, and sales practices often lead to major penalties and lawsuits.

- Heed whistle-blowers who try to alert management to hidden problems or dangers.

- Early warnings of impending crises go unnoticed for a number of reasons, including underestimation of the problem, hubris, and a failure to connect the dots.

- Companies increase the likelihood of heeding the warning signs of crises when they empower employees, make sure that someone in authority is alert to their warnings, and establish core crisis teams.

5

Containment

*Preventing a Bad Situation
from Becoming Worse*

Key Topics Covered in This Chapter

- *Rule 1: Use quick and decisive action*

- *Rule 2: Put people first*

- *Rule 3: Be physically at the scene*

- *Rule 4: Communicate liberally*

LEFT UNCHECKED, some crises will move from bad to worse. This is what happened during the pedophile scandal that rocked the Catholic diocese of Boston over a period of years. The more Church officials dithered and denied, the worse the situation became. A crisis in one area can also create crisis elsewhere if not checked promptly. For example, if embezzlement by a prominent executive is discovered, the media plays up the story. While management is occupied with the legal issues of the embezzlement, other bad things happen. Because of the damage done to the company's reputation, talented executives may be pirated by competitors, promising employee candidates are likely to take jobs elsewhere, and the company's sales reps will report that some key customers have shifted their orders to other suppliers. Meanwhile, outraged shareholders may even bring a lawsuit against board members, citing their failure to fulfill their fiduciary responsibilities.

This chapter offers four rules for containing a crisis once it is recognized. *Crisis containment* is defined here as the decisions and actions that aim to keep a crisis from growing worse.

Crisis containment has a lot in common with the work of emergency medical technicians (EMTs)—namely, to stabilize the situation until more decisive action can be mounted, as in the following example:

An EMT van has just arrived at the scene of a traffic accident. The driver of one of the vehicles is breathing and semiconscious but already in shock. He is also bleeding heavily from a laceration to his arm. There are no other visible signs of injury.

The EMTs know at a glance that this driver is in grave danger from blood loss, from shock, and from any internal injuries that they are not equipped to detect or treat. Their job is clear: to keep the crash victim's condition from worsening while they rush him to the hospital. Once there, doctors and nurses will take the steps necessary to restore this driver to health. So the EMTs load the victim into the van, and one drives while the other applies a pressure bandage to the arm wound and takes steps to prevent the patient from going into shock.

The EMTs in that example are practicing crisis containment. When crisis strikes your company, think like an EMT. Identify the problem, and then figure out what you can do to stabilize the situation and prevent the crisis from growing worse. This stop-gap action will give your crisis team time to implement an appropriate contingency plan.

Rule 1: Act Quickly and Decisively

Above all, observe the first rule of crisis containment, which is to act quickly and decisively. This is what Johnson & Johnson (J&J) officials did back in 1982 when the first ties between customer illness and fatalities were associated with Tylenol, the company's market-dominating, nonprescription painkiller. Within a three-day period, seven people died after using Tylenol—all victims of a pharma-terrorist who planted cyanide-laced capsules in bottles of the product. How many tampered bottles were out there? Would more die? Would copycat felons strike elsewhere in the country? Company officials had no way to answer those questions, so they acted decisively, withdrawing all Tylenol products from drugstore shelves—all 22 million bottles. And they kept the product off store shelves until they had developed a tamper-proof container in which they and the public had confidence. This action cost J&J hundreds of million of dollars in the short term but contained the crisis and made it possible for the brand to regain its stature and profitability in the long term. That swift action prevented a criminal act from further undermining public confidence in Johnson & Johnson's global enterprise and its many products.

The Johnson & Johnson case underscores the importance of act-ing quickly and decisively in crisis situations. This is more easily said than done. Good managers know that quality decisions depend on having a solid base of information and sound analysis of the situa-tion. But both are usually absent in a crisis. Information is limited, and you don't have time to gather as much as you need. And what-ever action you take is likely to be costly and expose your interven-tion to lots of second-guessing once the crisis has passed.

Limited information in most cases should not prevent a rapid re-sponse, particularly if the contingency planning recommended ear-lier has been done. For example, if someone smells smoke in our building, we don't have to know the extent of the fire or where it is located in order to act. We act immediately to evacuate the building and call the fire department. If we've practiced contingency plan-ning, the fire department's phone number will be on our speed-dial, and every employee will have been trained in rapid evacuation of the building. Should we worry about a false alarm? No. We should know in advance that most building evacuations are based on false alarms. But the cost of a false alarm is nothing compared to the cost of multiple deaths and the property damage caused by a fire that may occur if evacuation is delayed.

Rule 2: Put People First

The Johnson & Johnson Tylenol case and the example of a fire emergency illustrate the second rule of crisis containment: Make people your first concern. In the end, material things can be re-placed—and most are already insured against loss—as in this case:

> *A torrential rainstorm caused serious water damage to a section of an office building, destroying electronic equipment, carpeting, paper records, and the work space used by ten employees on the ground floor. Robert, the office manager, was on the scene the next morning as employees showed up for work. He helped those employees and a hired crew clean up the area and dry it out. Within twenty-four hours the place was ready for business once again.*

Three days later, several employees complained of breathing problems and headaches. Many suspected that the carpeting was to blame. Though it had been thoroughly cleaned and dried after the flood, many believed that the carpet was infested with mold. The manager thought about his options. He could have the carpet cleaned again and hope that the problem would go away. He could put in a request to have the carpet replaced, but that would involve waiting several days for budget approval and still more for installation. Instead, Robert ordered all carpeting in the area to be removed and replaced. "I'll worry about the cost later," he told himself.

Robert's approach in that case satisfied the first and second rules of crisis containment: He acted quickly and decisively, and he put people above material goods. By replacing the suspicious carpeting immediately he demonstrated that the health of employees was more important than any other consideration. Someone might later complain that the cost was not in the budget, but crisis costs are *never* in the budget. So within the bounds of good sense, don't worry about the budget or the other workplace procedures that govern how things are done under normal conditions. Instead, do what it takes to keep people safe.

Rule 3: Be on the Scene

The third rule of crisis containment is for top people to be physically on the scene as quickly as possible. A physical presence sends a loud and clear message that those people think the situation is extremely important. Their absence sends the opposite message, that they have other priorities at the moment. Think of the impact of this message on people affected by the crisis. As author and practitioner Laurence Barton bluntly put it, "People want to see their leaders in a crisis."[1] Here's what can happen when the people in charge choose to avoid the spotlight:

The sinking of the nuclear submarine Kursk in August 2000 was a major blow to the reputation and morale of the Russian Navy. To make

*matters worse, senior officials failed to mount a rescue mission and later
had to call on Western rivals to recover the ship. Still worse, 118 crew
members were lost.*

*The Russian government's handling of the crisis was equally inef-
fective. The Ministry of Defense initially downplayed the seriousness
of the incident, saying that the sub had merely run aground during a
training exercise. The crew, it told the public, was in no immediate danger. Later, as details began to leak out, the ministry spread rumors of a
collision with a NATO submarine. These pronouncements were proved
false as more information became available, indicating that the government was more interested in covering up the debacle than in resolving it
and saving the crew.*

*The sinking of the Kursk was also an enormous public relations
blunder for President Vladimir Putin. Putin, who was vacationing at a
southern Russia resort at the time, appeared in casual clothes to tell the
television audience that the situation was under control. He then disap-
peared for several days. His failure to take a personal hand in managing
the crisis angered the public and outraged families of the ill-fated crew.
As reported by the* Los Angeles Times, *"Putin seemed aloof and dis-
tant after the* Kursk *sank. He stayed on vacation for nearly a week at
the Black Sea resort of Sochi and didn't request foreign rescuers until
August 16. Instead of going to the submarine's Arctic port to energize
rescue efforts, he portrayed himself last week as a functionary who didn't
want to get in the way."*[2] *Eventually, the Russian leader found time
to visit the* Kursk's *home base, where he was greeted by a hostile
and angry crowd.*

You can almost forgive Vladimir Putin for failing to observe
Rule 3 of crisis containment. After all, his background as a KGB official had not prepared him for handling anything like this. The term
public relations probably wasn't even in the secretive KGB's vocabu-
lary. It's less easy to forgive Western executives for making this mistake. But they break this rule just the same. One example was
Exxon's CEO Lawrence Rawls, who didn't appear at the site of the
disastrous *Exxon Valdez* accident for three weeks after the event had
taken place.[3] Instead of sending its top person to the scene of his-

tory's biggest and most damaging oil spill, Exxon sent a district functionary. The example set by New York City Mayor Rudy Giuliani
stands in sharp contrast to Russia's Putin and Exxon's Rawls. Giuliani seemed omnipresent in the aftermath of the 9/11 disaster. He
was on the scene within minutes of the terrorist strikes against the
Twin Towers, in command, available to the press, and present at
dozen of funerals in the weeks that followed.

This is not to say that a CEO must take command of every crisis. For example, the head of a huge retail chain such as Home Depot
should not feel compelled to rush to the scene of a store fire. That
would be nice, but not strictly necessary. The local or district manager could fill the same role. The response should be proportional to
the crisis. On the other hand, if the store fire killed customers or employees, the crisis level would demand the presence of the CEO.

Rule 4: Communicate Liberally

Fires, power outages, hostile takeovers, major product failures, and
other damaging events create a sudden and substantial demand for
information. People want to know what happened, how it happened, what will happen next, and how they should respond. Rule 4
of crisis containment requires that those questions be answered to
the extent that answers are available.

Every contingency plan and every crisis management team
should have a communication plan at the ready to provide information as it become available. Obviously, that plan cannot have a stock
set of answers for people's questions, but it can and should have all
the mechanisms for communicating in place. These include:

- A blueprint for gathering available facts

- A designated spokesperson

- The names and phone numbers of the people and institutions
  that should be contacted in the wake of a crisis (managers,
  supervisors, fire and police, the media, and so forth)

- An information hot line that people can call for information and instructions

- A single group e-mail address that can send a message to all employees and directors at once

- An off-site communications center equipped with phones, cell phones, and Internet connections (being off-site is important in the case of a building fire; cell phones are important because landlines might not be working)

Do you have a communication plan in place? Would it meet the requirements of a serious crisis?

Counter Rumors and Speculation with Facts

A sudden crisis creates an information vacuum. Something has happened, but no one knows what—at least initially. People are hungry for information. Just as nature abhors a vacuum, empty information space tends to fill itself with whatever comes along, even if it is nothing more than speculation and rumor. If you have any doubts about this, turn on your television or radio the next time there is a major catastrophe, the outbreak of war, or a political scandal. Broadcasters go into full-time coverage mode for such events and bring in all their talking heads to fill airtime. In the early stages, most discourse is pure speculation, since broadcasters will say just about anything to fill dead airtime. During the first day of the Clinton-Lewinsky scandal, for example, a fact-deprived political reporter for National Public Radio struggled desperately for something to say about the salacious scandal's impact on Clinton's political future. "People are saying . . . ," she intoned, indicating that even the legitimate media had plunged deep into the rumor barrel.

The fourth rule of crisis containment is to communicate the facts that exist—no more, no less. Doing so will help fill the information vacuum, leaving less space for rumor and speculation. A good communicator can also dampen rumors directly as in these examples:

A number of employees are concerned that our proposed merger with Oscar's Cat Food, Inc. will result in closure of our Nashville regional plant. This concern is unfounded. I can tell you that there are no plans to close the Nashville plant.

As many have speculated, the fire of October 27 caused considerable damage to our information systems equipment. The full extent of that damage is currently being accessed. In the meantime, our off-site backup system is fully operational and capable of handling all of our information and transaction requirements during the recovery period. Beginning tomorrow, all orders will be channeled through our Limerick, Ireland, customer service center, processed by the off-site data center, and filled by our regional distribution facilities.

Several recent news stories have reported alleged improprieties in the management of your company's employee pension plan. At this point, none of the allegations have been substantiated. The board of directors has engaged an independent audit firm, Farnsworth & Farrell, to conduct a thorough investigation, which is now in its early stages. A full report is anticipated in early November of this year and will be made available to all. Any interim findings will be communicated to you without delay.

As you communicate, get out all the bad news at once. It is better and more honest to do this than to release a continuing stream of bad news. Putting out all the bad news at once is similar to quickly pulling off a bandage. It hurts for a moment, but then the hurt goes away. Likewise, once all the bad news is out, subsequent communications are likely to be dominated by good news. For example:

We are please to report that a review of fire damage at our data center by IT Vice President Jane Harley and COO Jake Newhall found that losses are much less serious than anticipated, and that the system will be up and running sooner than earlier believed. Meanwhile, the off-site backup system is in its second day of processing customer orders and is doing so without a hitch!

Speak with One Voice

Even though your crisis management team may have chosen a spokesperson to communicate with the media, the media is likely to seek out others for their stories and opinions. For example, if a senior manager has just been slapped with a sexual harassment lawsuit, female employees are likely to get phone calls at work and at home from reporters seeking a good story. These employees may or may not be in command of the facts. And what they say could make matters worse. So encourage employees to refer all inquiries to the company spokesperson.

Communicate with Stakeholders and the Public

In containing a crisis, employees are a natural first concern. But do not forget about other stakeholders: shareholders, suppliers, customers, and strategic business partners, among others. They will want to know what's going on and what to expect. The same goes for the public in the geographic areas where your company operates. Give the public the same facts that you give to your employees and stakeholders; a press release is often the quickest and best approach.

Remember too that what you say and how you say it are both critical. The way you communicate may precipitate actions that can make the crises worse—or better. A crisis, by definition, means that there is bad news. Dealing with pain and anger early can forestall far worse problems later on. Your goal is to contain the overall crisis, not to make the present moment easier.

When in Doubt, Let Your Training, Values, and Instincts Guide You

Crisis containment can strain a person's capacity to make good decisions. Facts are few, and decision makers must act swiftly or risk a still greater crisis situation. There is no time to gather more information,

calmly consider alternative responses, or think about the unanticipated consequences of each response. Think for a moment of what it
must be like to be a 23-year-old lieutenant whose infantry platoon
has just walked into an ambush. Two men are already hit, and everyone else is pinned down by withering fire from two directions—or
is it three? The heavy undergrowth makes it impossible to see what
you're up against. The noise is deafening and everyone's scared, including you. You know that if you stay put, enemy mortars will have
time to zero in. If you move, your men will be exposed. The platoon
sergeant crawls to within shouting distance: "What are we gonna do,
sir?" Yes, what are you going to do?

If you are charged with containing a dangerous crisis, you and
the young lieutenant have much in common. Little information is
available, and the situation is desperate. But you cannot allow indeci-
sion to paralyze you; you must act and act quickly, before the situation becomes worse. If the right thing to do isn't apparent, do this:

- **Fall back on your planning and training.** If you've done contingency planning, you will already have thought through how
  best to respond to a range of potential problems. And if you
  tested your plans with simulations and training exercises, you'll
  have a set of viable options for immediate action.

Seek Out Wise Counsel

If you must make an important decision quickly and with insuf-
ficient information, don't feel that you must do it alone; seek
the counsel of people you trust. Ideally, your crisis management
team includes trustworthy people who think clearly in difficult
situations. Perhaps simulations have prepared you to work together under stressful conditions. If you don't have such a team,
keep in touch with a wise and trusted friend or mentor—a person you can rely on to objectively critique your ideas and provide good advice. Test your ideas with those counselors. They
have experienced similar situations. They may suggest alternative courses of action that you have failed to consider.

- **Let your values guide you.** Your ethical sense of right and wrong is a powerful compass. If the landscape is murky, take your direction from your values.

- **Listen to your instincts.** If something feels wrong, it probably *is* wrong. Don't do it.

Summing Up

- Observe the four rules of crisis containment:

  1. **Act quickly and decisively.** Delay will only allow the situation to grow worse.

  2. **Put people first.** Building, inventory, credit rates, and corporate reputations can all be recouped; the lives of customers and employees cannot.

  3. **Get top people to the crisis scene as quickly as possible.** This will demonstrate that the crisis is being taken seriously.

  4. **Communicate liberally.** This is the best way to counter rumors and speculation.

- When the right course of action is not clear, let your training, your values, and your instincts guide you.

6

Crisis Resolution

The Road to Recovery

Key Topics Covered in This Chapter

- *The importance of moving quickly and decisively*

- *The role of communications*

- *How project management techniques can help in crisis resolution*

- *Why strong leadership matters*

I F YOU'VE FOLLOWED the rules of containment offered earlier, your company will be in a much better position to resolve its crisis. Fast and effective action on the containment front will result in a crisis that is smaller and more manageable. The containment effort will also assure that the true problem and its dimensions are correctly identified. Otherwise, crisis resolution will be fighting the wrong battle. Beyond the containment phase, the job of the crisis management team is to keep on top of the problem and not let up until it is resolved and the situation has returned to normalcy.

This chapter will take you through the many things the crisis management team must do to bring about a resolution.

Move Quickly

Time is not your friend during a crisis. As in the containment phase, time only gives the problem an opportunity to spread and take root, making it more intractable. The containment effort is a holding action at best; delay in working toward a resolution provides opportunities for the crisis to break through that holding action. Consider this hypothetical news report:

> As the strike against Amalgamated Hat Racks enters its third week, a nationwide boycott of Amalgamated's products appears to be taking shape. Jessie Jamison, a spokesperson for the striking union, announced today that union members across the country are being asked to boycott all Amalgamated outlets and products. "In all likelihood," said Jamison,

"we'll have pickets around the company's retail stores in Toronto, Boston, Los Angeles, and Santa Fe by this time next week."

A long-lasting crisis may also imprint the public consciousness with a negative view of the company. If the morning newspaper reports your company's travails day after day and week after week, the public will associate the company with trouble and conflict for years to come. Microsoft's long-running battle with the U.S. Department of Justice over whether it was guilty of monopolistic practices—and subsequent battles with several state prosecutors—certainly had that

---

Tips for Relieving Crisis Stress

If you are on a crisis management team, you will feel lots of pressure. The pace is fast. The stakes are high—for the company, for your fellow employees, and for you personally. Because your control of the facts is incomplete, you know that mistakes are easy to make. Fear is in the air. The people around you are nervous and unsettled, and their emotions are bound to infect you.

Here are a few tips for relieving the stress:

- Get enough sleep.

- Take a break and do anything that will dissipate the tension building up inside you: a long walk in the woods, a bike ride along the seashore. If you play a musical instrument, play a few tunes every day.

- Don't fixate on what could go wrong. Instead, look at risks objectively, and then shift your focus to the benefits of making things go right.

- Avoid a bunker mentality. Spend more time with "normal" people—i.e., people who are not in the midst of a crisis.

Remember that some tension is good; it will keep you focused and keep your energy level up. Too much tension, on the other hand, may paralyze your ability to think and act.

effect. The public was treated to regular reports of Microsoft's alleged sins. Even those found later to be groundless surely had an impact on the public's attitude toward the software giant.

Equally bad, it's unlikely that your business will operate at peak efficiency as long as the crisis continues. Suppliers and customers will be wary. Employee defections will increase, and recruiting efforts will be more difficult. Employees will waste time as they worry about their jobs or speculate among themselves about the company's problems. The antidote to these negative effects is to resolve the crisis as quickly as possible.

Gather Facts Continually

Crises are often dynamic events, mutating on their own or in response to the action of participants. You may begin resolution efforts with a very clear picture of the problems and the forces arrayed against you. That picture is likely to change in response to whatever actions you take or fail to take. Also, new information will become available during every day of the crisis.

The remedy to both problems—incomplete information and a shifting situation—is to continually gather and process facts about the crisis as you attempt to resolve it. Make "What new things have we learned today?" part of daily crisis team meetings. Adopt a sense-and-respond model in which you are continually adapting to new information. To do otherwise—that is, to hold to a plan based on initial facts—can only assure failure.

Communicate Relentlessly

Communication is one of the crisis team's most essential tools. Telling the company's story provides important information for key constituents, including customers, suppliers, shareholders, and employees. Communication is also a means of suppressing rumors and coordinating the many activities required to resolve the crisis. For

Tips for Communicating During a Crisis

- Be candid.

- Give the facts.

- Be honest about what you know *and* what you don't know.

- Set up a rumor control hot line.

- Record a voice message on the company information line every day with the latest information.

- Don't speculate.

Note: The subject of communication—particularly with the media—is so important that it is treated separately later.

example, in the aftermath of a fire or storm, employees must be told when and where to report for work and what they should do. If the information system is down for the count, someone must notify creditors that their payments may be late. If picket lines are preventing the production facility from filling customer orders, those customers should hear from you. If news reporters are knocking on the door, you must have a strategy for getting your side of the story across and making it resonate with the public.

If you've created a communication plan as part of normal contingency planning, as recommended earlier, you'll be ready for most eventualities in this area. If you have not, appropriate members of the crisis management team should quickly develop one.

Document Your Actions

Document your sources of information as well as your decisions, intentions, and actions throughout the course of crisis resolution. You may question the value of that advice. After all, how many generals ask their staffs to chronicle their campaigns as they happen? Who has the time when so much is happening around them?

In fact, military organizations do chronicle their decisions and actions. Doing so provides a record from which after-action lessons can be drawn. At the beginning of World War II, for example, the U.S. Navy assigned Harvard historian Samuel Eliot Morison, a high-ranking naval reserve officer, to the task of chronicling the war at sea from beginning to end. Morison, in turn, recruited a staff of researchers to help with the project. Their collective effort produced a fifteen-volume work from which the next two generations of naval students, strategists, and tacticians would draw important lessons.

Documenting your situation and actions will have similar value in the aftermath of crisis, when the crisis team and others attempt to learn what went well, what went badly, and how they can improve in the future. Documentation will also be helpful in any subsequent legal actions.

Use Project Management Techniques When Appropriate

The difficulties you face in resolving a crisis may be qualitatively similar to the challenges you face in other areas of your business. Examples include launching a new product into a new market, re-organizing an operating unit, and building an e-commerce function. Such challenges are often addressed through formal project teams. Crises and projects share several important characteristics:

- They are nonroutine, rarely repeating activities.

- They require the skills and experience of people from many different functions.

- They are not scheduled to continue indefinitely but are to be resolved at some future date.

- Participants return to their regular duties once the job is finished.

Those characteristics suggest that crisis teams should organize themselves and attack problems as project teams already do with considerable success. That means bringing together the experiences, authority, and skills needed to gain control of the situation. However, there are some notable differences. Crisis teams, unlike project teams, do not always have the luxury of time in which to plan their work. Teams formed around specific threats identified through risk auditing (e.g., fire, flood, or a breakdown of IT systems) have contingency plans, and many have used simulations to train. But even these lack certain knowledge of what must be done because crises often evolve in unpredictable ways. Nevertheless, there are enough similarities to encourage crisis managers to take a page from the project manager's book.

Project management has four essential phases: defining and organizing, planning, managing execution, and closing down the project. Let's consider how crisis managers can adapt those steps to their own challenges.

Defining and Organizing

The tasks involved in the first phase are to clearly define the project's objectives and to organize the right people and resources around them. Whether crisis managers are facing a product recall or the aftermath of a disastrous fire, they can do the same, asking "What—exactly—is the problem? What must we do to resolve it? Who should we enlist to help us? What resources will we need to solve the problem and return our situation to normal?"

If you define the crisis correctly and organize the right set of people and resource around it, you will have made an excellent beginning.

Planning

Planning begins with the objective and works backward in four successive steps:

1. Identifying each of the many tasks that must be done

2. Identifying the individuals or groups best qualified to accomplish each task

3. Estimating the time required to complete each task

4. Scheduling all tasks in the right order

If fire damage to your office building is the source of crisis, your objective might be three-fold: secure temporary office space for dislocated workers as needed; restore the damaged space to working order; and communicate regularly with affected personnel. Approached from a project management perspective, each of those objectives would then be broken down into a necessary set of tasks and subtasks. For example, to restore the damaged space you might identify the following tasks and estimate the time required to complete them:

- Obtain a complete evaluation of the fire damage and itemized list of necessary repairs (fourteen days).

- Negotiate with and hire a contractor to do the repairs (fourteen days).

- Work with an office-furniture supplier and technology vendor to refit the repaired space (thirty days).

- Oversee the contractor's reconstruction work (eighteen days).

- Communicate with employees about building restoration progress (ongoing).

Some of those tasks must be tackled in a sequence; for example, you cannot negotiate with a contractor until the damages have been assessed. Other tasks can be handled in parallel; for example, you can be working with an office-furniture supplier even as repairs are being made.

The planning process must also assign responsibility for each task to a specific individual. Assigning individual responsibility is your best assurance that tasks will be done and done well. If no one in particular owns a task, it probably won't be done on time or to your satisfaction.

Managing Execution

The managing execution phase requires all the traditional chores of effective management as well as careful monitoring and control. Together, they assure adherence to the plan, standards, and the budget. The budget is rarely an issue during a crisis. The company is usually taking such a financial beating that the cost of efforts to stem the losses and get things back on track pales by comparison. Monitoring and control, however, remain critical. Always ask these questions:

- Are all planned tasks under way?

- Are all tasks on schedule, or have some hit obstacles?

- Are the company's messages to employees, the media, and other stakeholders accurate and consistent?

Project leaders spend most of their time coordinating the efforts of their teams. Crisis team leaders must do the same. They need everyone working together and at a high level of energy to defeat the crisis.

Just a reminder: The tools of project management are not appropriate in resolving all crises. A deepening financial crisis is one; a case of fraud or embezzlement is another. However, when a damaging event hits and quickly ends—as in a fire, a paralyzing blizzard, or a product recall—project management tools can help you pick up the pieces and return operations to normal in an orderly way.

Closing Down the Project

One common feature of projects and crises is that they eventually end. The end of a project is the point at which its objectives are achieved. The new product line is launched. The new e-commerce Web site is up and running successfully. The company's move to a new headquarters is finished, and the pace of business has returned to normal. A project terminates when its objectives are met, but that happens only after wrapping up loose ends and reflecting on the lessons learned from the project.

Crisis management likewise has a final, wrap-up phase, and one of the main tasks of that phase is to look back on the experience and draw out its lessons: What went right? What did we do wrong? How would we change our approach if and when another similar crisis hits the company? The learning issue will be addressed in detail later. The points to remember here are that the crisis team must

Don't Play the Blame Game

As a crisis heats up and people try to determine what went wrong, the impulse to blame someone becomes almost irresistible. Certainly, a team member's incompetence or serious error may have caused the crisis. In the meltdown of Enron, for example, fingers pointed to Chief Financial Officer Andrew Fastow and Chairman and CEO Kenneth Lay. Finger-pointing, however, did nothing to rescue the company, save the jobs of thousands of honest and competent employees, or salvage the equity of shareholders. Energy spent on finding a villain or scapegoat is counterproductive during a crisis period. It lowers morale and stifles the creativity and commitment you need to solve the problem. So instead of playing the blame game, create an atmosphere in which people look forward to what needs to be done, not backward to who was at fault. There will be plenty of time in the aftermath to deal with blame.

- declare an official end to the crisis—but do not be premature;

- document everything significant that happened;

- get participants to participate in a postmortem, which is your best assurance that the organization will learn from its expensive experience.

Be a Leader

During periods of crisis, people look to a strong leader. They don't look to committees or to teams as much as to a confident, visibly engaged leader to pull them through the fray. This is why military commanders mingle with their troops on the front lines of battles. This is why Winston Churchill was so often seen on the streets of London during the terrifying weeks of the blitz. This is why Lee

Iacocca, during the 1980s campaign to save Chrysler Corporation from extinction, made himself into a household name in North America. Iacocca seemed to be everywhere as he struggled to secure government guarantees for the loans Chrysler needed to rebuild itself. It seemed that wherever you turned—from the evening news, to *BusinessWeek*, to a series of television ads—Iacocca was there, telling people why a renewed Chrysler Corporation was good for jobs, the economy, and American competitiveness. Leaders like Iacocca who demonstrate strength, commitment, and confidence infect others with the same qualities.

The importance of leader visibility cannot be overstated. In his study of the 9/11 tragedy in New York City, Paul Argenti found that the most effective crisis managers displayed high levels of visibility.

> *They understood that a central part of their job is political and that their employees are, in a very real sense, their constituents. In periods of upheaval, workers want concrete evidence that top management views their distress as one of the company's key concerns. Written statements have their place, but oral statements and the sound of an empathetic human voice communicate sincerity. And if the voice belongs to a company leader, the listener has reason to think that the full weight of the company stands behind whatever promises or assurances are being made.*[1]

Perhaps no contemporary leader provided the level of visibility advocated by Argenti more effectively than New York City's former mayor, Rudolph Giuliani. Giuliani appeared at the scene of the 9/11 attacks within minutes, where he took charge of rescue operations. After the Twin Towers fell, he remained on the scene. The man seemed to be everywhere: at press conferences, at a string of funeral services, at the crisis command center, on phone interviews, talking with people on the street. As Argenti put it, "[Giuliani's] visibility, combined with his decisiveness, candor, and compassion, lifted the spirits of all New Yorkers—indeed, of all Americans."[2]

If it's your lot to lead during a crisis, play your part well. Whether you are the CEO of a large corporation or a department supervisor, find out as quickly as possible what the real problem is. Sift through the rumors, hearsay, and irrelevant information until you find the

When Leadership Is the Problem

Current leadership is the problem in some situations. This was the case in 1999 when an investigation revealed that the Salt Lake Olympic Committee (SLOC) was involved in a network of corruption. Its members had allegedly supplied thirteen International Olympic Committee (IOC) members with scholarships, cash, and various lavish gifts in return for their votes to award the 2002 Winter Olympics to Salt Lake City, Utah. Of the thirteen, four resigned from the IOC, five were suspended, and one was given a warning. The other two members of the Salt Lake City group, the president/CEO and the vice president, also resigned. The SLOC scandal rocked the world of Olympic sports and threatened the 2002 Winter Games. It was the most serious crisis faced by any modern Olympic event.

With its leadership banished and its reputation deeply tarnished, raising the $1.4 billion in private funding needed to host the games would be extremely difficult. Wisely, Utah's governor appointed an outsider—Boston-area businessman Mitt Romney—to assume leadership and reverse the SLOC's flagging fortunes. Romney was a new face and was untainted by the problems associated with his predecessors. He was also a successful venture capitalist and business consultant with experience in turning around troubled companies. Better still, he had exactly what the SLOC lacked, a reputation for effectiveness and high ethical standards. That reputation was needed to attract the private funding and volunteers needed to make the 2002 Winter Games a success.

Romney's success in steering the SLOC out of its crisis and putting on a successful and memorable ten days of winter sporting events is a clear reminder of the importance of effective and respected leadership during crisis. If a distressed organization lacks that kind of leadership, it must dismiss its current leaders and bring in others.

truth. You can do that by asking the right people, listening to the most reliable voices, and going to the right places. And once you know the truth, respond by

- Being visible—demonstrating that someone is in charge and working to make things better

- Facing the crisis—turning fear into positive action

- Being vigilant—watching for new developments and recognizing the importance of new information

- Maintaining a focus on the company's priorities—ensuring that people are safe first, and then addressing the next most critical needs

- Assessing and responding to what is in your control—and ignoring what is not

- Breaking the rules when necessary—rules, budgets, and policies are seldom made with crises in mind

And don't forget to get people working together. A leader has the power to draw people together to act as a team. The very fact that they are doing something useful will help relieve tension, reduce fear, and resolve the crisis. Consider this example:

A catalog retailer offered a large number of custom products—monogrammed bags, sweaters, and so forth—in its holiday catalog. But it totally underestimated the response. From the moment the catalog was released in October, the company's phone lines were swamped with orders. The company found itself in an unusual crisis: It was buried under a mountain of orders that had to be processed and shipped in time for the holidays. It hired temporary workers to help with the laborious job of customizing and shipping, but not enough reliable temps were available to deal with the order backlog.

The head of distribution recognized that if they didn't get everything shipped in time for Christmas, there might not be a next season. So the CEO put out a call for help. He recruited managers and staff personnel to work evening shifts in the warehouse—after they had done their regular jobs. This was a hardship for many, especially for those who had children at home. But the CEO did such a good job of explaining the details and gravity of the situation, and how their contributions would help resolve it, that most people volunteered for two or three evening shifts each week.

Everyone—from the CEO down—worked together for six long and grueling weeks. And their extraordinary team effort got the job done. The company enjoyed an astonishing 80 percent growth in sales that year. What could have been a crisis and failure was turned around by teamwork. And leadership made it possible.

Getting people back into their normal routines can be one of the most important contributions a leader can make. Returning to work has many therapeutic effects. It takes the edge off the anxiety that employees experience when they have nothing to do but sit, wait, and wonder. It eliminates opportunities for idle speculation, gossip, and rumors. (Remember, idle hands *are* the devil's workshop.) Most important, it gives people a real feeling that they are part of the solution and that they are making things better.

Declare the End of the Crisis

At some point, a crisis must come to an end. But at what point does one declare that it's over? For long-struggling and bankrupt Polaroid Corporation, the innovator of instant photography, its crisis ended in July 2002, when an affiliate of One Equity Partners acquired the company's assets. The end of other business crises are less clear cut. For example, Malden Mills, a family-owned textile producer and developer of Polartec, declared bankruptcy in November 2001 after years of struggling against overseas competition. The owner, Aaron Feuerstein, won a reprieve for his company in late 2003 by engineering a financing arrangement with a real estate development company. In return for a sizable cash infusion to the business, the developer would be able to build six hundred units of rental housing on surplus property owned by Malden Mills. It would also share ownership of the company with Feuerstein. But the crisis wasn't entirely over. Feuerstein would have to find more than $100 million to buy out the developer's interest and get his company back. The first stage of Malden Mills's crisis had ended, but a second had begun.

How can you tell when a crisis is over? Look for these signs:

- Employees are back to their normal routines.

- Customers and suppliers have the confidence they need to do business with your company.

- The telephone rings and it is *not* a news reporter.

- Sales, earnings, and other metrics of business performance are back on track.

Those are signs that the crisis is over and that management can redirect its attention to its primary responsibilities: growth and profits.

Summing Up

- Time is not your friend during a crisis. Every day that a crisis continues creates a negative image for the company and provides opportunities for that image to spread. So once you've contained the crisis, move quickly and decisively to resolve it.

- The facts of the crisis will change as it is resolved. So continue to gather information. Doing so will keep a clear picture of the situation in front of the crisis team.

- Relentless communication will provide information to key stakeholders and suppress rumors and speculation.

- Document the crisis and its resolution as you move forward; doing so will make it possible to later evaluate the crisis team's performance and to learn from the experience.

- Many crises can be resolved using crisis management techniques, which include defining the objective, planning, managing execution, and closing down the project.

- People look to leaders for strong, confident, and visible leadership during periods of crisis.

7

Mastering the Media

Make It Your Story

Key Topics Covered in This Chapter

- *Suggestions for dealing with print and electronic media*

- *The principle of audience segmentation*

- *Using segmentation to create a systematic communication strategy*

- *Frequently asked questions about crisis communications*

OMMUNICATION is an important tool for every crisis handler and in each active stage of crisis management: contingency planning, containment, and resolution. Its importance as an instrument of control and coordination has been emphasized in previous chapters. Communication through the media—newspapers, television, and radio—must also be used to accurately frame the crisis in the public's mind. Fail to deal with the media effectively, and your side of the story may never be heard. Worse, your company's reputation may be publicly attacked by a hostile or misinformed reporter or news editor.

This chapter offers suggestions for making your dealings with the media more collaborative and effective.

Handle the Media with Care

Give intense attention to how you communicate with the public through the media. Your messages should be accurate and candid. They should also represent your point of view and include facts that support it. If you get your messages out early and often, there is a good chance that you will successfully frame the story in the public's mind. What do we mean by "framing"? Consider the hypothetical case of a chemical plant explosion. Based on all available information, management concluded the following:

The cause of the explosion was a failed pressure valve. That valve, like all others in the plant, was regularly inspected. Records indicate that the most recent inspection of the failed valve revealed no problems. Further, the chemical leak resulting from the explosion was contained by the plant's built-in safeguards. The public was never endangered. This was the first such leak in the plant's twenty-two-year history.

If the company were to get this story out quickly, most of the public would frame the situation in the terms cited above. If the company failed to disseminate that information, however, the media might spin the story in a much different way. Consider one possible newspaper account of the same story:

An explosion at Acme Chemical's Manchester plant released an un-known quantity of toxic substances last night. The incident is one of a string of mishaps that have afflicted U.K. chemical plants—the most recent being a March 12 accident in Liverpool that killed one employee and forced hundreds to evacuate their homes in the dead of night.

Six hundred people live near the Acme plant. Nigel Bentley is one of them. "It's a bit frightening, isn't it?" Mr. Bentley told our reporter. "There's no telling what's going on over there. We could have another Bhopal disaster right here in Manchester." (The Bhopal, India, disaster of 1984 killed more than seven thousand and injured thousands more.)

Mr. Bentley's concern raises a larger question: How safe are Britons from plants like Acme's?

Notice how the newspaper account frames the story in terms of a larger concern with chemical industry safety within the United Kingdom, citing a deadly accident at another company's plant. And without any reference to actual endangerment by Acme's plant, it uses the comment of one uninformed neighbor and a reference to the Bhopal catastrophe to inject an element of imminent danger. This framing of the story is much different than the one issued by company managers. Not coincidentally, it is more likely to sell newspapers.

The newspaper's framing of the issue will be the one that sticks in the public's mind if management drags its feet in communicating its side of the story. If that happens, Acme will have to shift its communication strategy from telling its story to refuting the news account—an uphill battle it is likely to lose.

Give Them the Facts

Reporters are neither ogres nor liars. They are simply interested in getting a story—hopefully, one that will give them a front-page by-line. Thus, if you delay issuing a statement or say, "No comment" or "We're studying the situation" to inquiring reporters, you will force them to define the story as best they can without your assistance. And you may not like what you read or see on television the next day. Crisis consultant and author Steven Fink put it this way: "No matter how good your crisis management team is, no matter how complete your crisis management plan, if you cannot communicate your message during a crisis, you have failed."[1]

One way to get across the story you want told is to (1) anticipate the questions that news reporters are likely to ask and (2) make a list of the five questions you would *least* like to be asked and then be prepared to answer them. Be assured that someone *will* ask those difficult questions. By anticipating media questions, you can form and articulate clear, complete responses that present your side of the story. In doing this you'll accomplish two things: First, you'll demonstrate that you have nothing to hide; second, you'll provide media representatives with the facts and supporting material they need to develop a decent and accurate story—and one that mirrors yours. Consider the following example:

> *Johnstone Machine Works has announced its plan to close a three-hundred-employee plant in the small town of Farmvale and consolidate its operations in a newer, larger plant located in a city several hundred miles away. It has invited the local media to a press conference. Wisely, Johnstone's public spokesperson and several other managers have anticipated and developed succinct but complete answers to the questions most likely to be asked.*

> *Question: Is it true that you'll be closing your plant in Farmvale?*
> *Wrong answer: Yes, we anticipate closing next May.*
> *Right answer: Competition from low-wage countries requires that we operate as efficiently as possible. As a result, and regrettably, we will be closing the Farmvale plant in May. Many of its functions will be shifted*

*to a larger, more efficient plant in Wuthering Heights. We are offering
early retirement options to many workers, and will give others hiring
preference at the new jobs we are creating in Wuthering Heights.*

Question: *As Farmvale's largest employer, won't your action turn
that community into a ghost town?*
Wrong answer: *We don't think so. It can get along without us.*
Right answer: *As a member of the Farmvale community for more
than thirty years, we recognize the impact of our decision on the town
and its residents. But Farmvale has a diversified economy and will
gradually adjust to our departure. We will be doing two things to facili-
tate that adjustment. First, all displaced personnel will be offered training to increase their employability in the community; second, we are
actively seeking a buyer for the Farmvale plant—a manufacturer that
will provide high-wage future employment in the same location.*

Question: *But in the meantime, won't your decision to pull out put
a big hole in the local economy?*
Wrong answer: *We don't think so.*
Right answer: *By our calculation the impact will be fairly small.
Here's why: Older workers who take our early retirement offer will
immediately begin receiving pension benefits in lieu of paychecks—and
their health benefits will continue. The company will continue paying
property tax to Farmvale for as long as it owns the plant. And though
regular operations will cease in May, many current employees will be
staying on the payroll for six months or more to handle shutdown
operations.*

Notice in that example how every question could have been anticipated. Notice too how the company spokesperson used every
question as an opportunity to tell Johnstone's story and to share fac-
tual information with the public. The spokesperson also gave the
questioner enough information to develop the core of his or her
story. In the absence of that information, a news reporter would have
had to develop the story through interviews with other people in
the community, people who might be poorly informed of the facts,
as in this example:

Local TV news report: This is Casper Jones reporting today from Farmvale, where Johnstone Machine Works, this community's largest employer, has just announced a plant closing. That closure will likely put three hundred employees out of work and possibly devastate the local economy. Here to share his views about the plant closure is Mr. Harley Bumpus, owner of a sporting goods store here in downtown Farmvale. Mr. Bumpus, tell us, what impact will Johnstone's plant closure have on your business and the rest of the town?

Mr. Bumpus: *This will put a lot of us out of business. Anytime you put three hundred people out of work in a town this size you've got big trouble. Who's gonna have the money to shop in my store or patronize the local restaurants—or pay their taxes for that matter? And with the manufacturing economy being what it is, I don't see another company coming in to provide employment.*

Reporter: *So it looks like a huge blow to this rural community?*

Mr. Bumpus: *You got that right.*

Reporter: *Well, that's how it looks from here. This is Casper Jones in Farmvale. Now back to our news anchor in Dubuque.*

Use the Right Spokesperson

Who should be the spokesperson? In most cases it should be the identifiable leader, usually the CEO. When the crisis involves highly technical issues on which the CEO is not a credible authority, consider a team approach to speaking with the media. In this team approach, the CEO provides context and an overview of the situation. He or she will then ask a more technically knowledgeable subordinate to fill in the details—in nontechnical terms, you hope. Anyone who watched the daily press briefings of the coalition forces during the Iraq war in the summer of 2003 may recall how U.S. Army General Tommy Franks, the top commander, began each session with a strategic overview and a few important highlights. Franks would then

Tips for Dealing with the Media

Remember that effective media relations begin *before* a crisis occurs.

One of the best ways to assure a fair hearing from newspapers, TV, and radio is to always treat their members in a respectful and professional way. If your company is like most, it has plenty of opportunities to interact with the media, particularly the print media, in noncrisis times: when earnings, executive promotions, and new products are announced; when the company seeks a variance from the local planning board; and so forth. Use those opportunities to build good relationships with reporters and earn their trust. Get to know them personally. When they come looking for a story, help them to the extent that you can. Do that, and they will be less likely to skewer the company when it stumbles. Here are a few more tips:

- Be prepared to deal with a blitzkrieg of phone calls once news of the crisis or event gets out.

- Be responsive. You will strengthen your relationship with the media if you recognize and respond to the fact that they are under real time pressures. So answer as many calls as you can. You'll be doing the reporters a favor, and a favor may be returned in how they report your story.

- Make the reporter's job easy. Reporters are under pressure to get a story and quickly turn it into a printable piece that day. So give them the facts, and outline the story for them. Do that, and there's a good chance the piece they write will be to your liking.

ask one of his direct reports to offer details of the war's progress in various sectors. For example, a U.S. Air Force commander would describe the previous night's bombing raids on Iraqi command-and-control infrastructure, a British general would report on his forces' experiences in areas assigned to them, and so forth. This team approach gave the presentation greater credibility and coherence.

Match the Message and Media
to Different Segments

The news conference setting described in the Johnstone example is a practical way to provide a set of messages to a broad audience, which in this and most other cases includes the following:

- Community leaders

- Employees

- Customers and suppliers

- Shareholders

- The general public

Alternatively, consider purchasing ad space in the print media to explain your side of the story. Corporations do this routinely when they want shareholders to vote a certain way in a takeover battle or when they simply want to communicate with the public. But don't rely on broad pronouncements to get your story across. News conferences, purchased space ads, and press releases are useful but cannot provide the details that interest particular segments of the audience. The best way to communicate those details is through a strategy that tailors your messages to discrete segments and delivers them through the most appropriate media.

Press releases have a place in crisis management and other forms of communications. Large companies rely on public relations personnel to write their press releases, but owners and managers of smaller companies generally must handle that chore themselves. Appendix B provides a primer on the basics of press-release writing.

Segment Your Audience

Audience segmentation is the basis of an effective communication strategy. Your company's marketing department doesn't rely on broad-based messages to raise awareness and interest in its products, does it? Surely not. Instead, it identifies key market segments and the unique concerns of each segment and then speaks to each in a suitable way and through a medium most likely to create high impact. You should adopt a similar segmentation practice as you communicate during a crisis.

So, as a first step, segment your audience by interests. For example, in the Johnstone/Farmvale case, employees will be very interested in the details of the plant closure that pertain to them exclusively: the company's early retirement plan, plans for severance pay, job retraining, opportunities to work in the new plant, and so forth. They will probably be much less interested in knowing the details of how the plant shutdown will impact Farmvale's tax base. Conversely, city officials will want to know everything about the tax base issue and the company's plans to find a buyer of its manufacturing facility, and less about others. Shareholders and suppliers will likewise have appetites for information specific to their interests. For example, shareholders will want to know how the plant closing and move will impact this year's earnings.

Once you've segmented your audience, you will have a better idea of the messages you need to develop and convey to each segment. You will, in fact, need to develop different messages for different audiences. Just be sure that those different messages are consistent and do not contradict one another.

Select the Most Appropriate Media

The second step in forming a communication strategy is to select the optimal media for getting your message to your chosen segments. If you wanted to contact five hundred registered users about a glitch in your company's new software program, would you place a notice in the *New York Times* or hold a press conference? Of course not. You would send each user a letter or e-mail apologizing for the problem and explaining how you intend to fix it. As a crisis communicator, you too must match the media to the audience. Do this by first answering these questions:

- With which audience segments should I communicate?

- Which are the best media for reaching each segment?

- What particular information will each segment value most?

TABLE 7-1

Segmented Communications Strategy

Segment	Key Messages	Media	Timing	Spokesperson(s)
Employees	• Jobs in new plant • Early retirement packages • Retraining program	• Companywide meeting • Letter to each employee	• Prior to press conference • Frequent follow-up	CEO, plant general manager, HR director
Customers	• Making changes to serve you better • Changes will make the company stronger • No disruption of orders or service	• Letter to all purchasing managers • Direct through sales reps • Industry trade magazines	• Concurrent with press release	VP of marketing
Suppliers	• Changes will make the company stronger	• Personal letter to all first- and second-tier suppliers • Personal calls to first-tier suppliers	• Immediately	Corporate supply-chain manager
Investors	• Full disclosure of the change, why and how it will make the company stronger	• Letter to shareholders • Webcast	• Immediately	CFO and VP of corporate investor relations
Community leaders	• Full disclosure of company plans and reasons for change • Special attention to employee and community concerns	• Meeting with community leaders	• Prior to press conference	CEO, plant general manager, HR director
Regulators, government agencies	• Full disclosure of company plans and reasons for change	• Registered letter	• Prior to press conference	COO, legal counsel
General public	• Full disclosure of company plans and reasons for change	• Press announcement	• After first speaking with key stakeholders	CEO, VP of corporate communications

Answers to those questions will guide you in determining with *whom* you must communicate, *what* you will say, and *how* you can best reach that audience segment. Table 7-1 indicates how Johnstone Machine Works might have segmented its different audiences and determined which messages and which means of communication would be most effective. Generally, it is the job of the corporate communications vice president to develop this strategy.

Be Systematic

The best time to develop a crisis communication strategy is *before* a crisis hits—as part of contingency planning for the many things that could go wrong. Depending on the type of business you operate, you would have a communication strategy for a product recall, a hostile takeover, a friendly merger, a natural or man-made disaster, and so forth. If you develop a strategy in anticipation of a potential problem, you have the time to investigate different media channels.

Frequently Asked Questions

Dealing with the media can be a nerve-wracking prospect, but it doesn't have to be. Follow the advice on handling the media with care and on matching your message to different segments, and you should be in good shape. And review these frequently asked questions; they're sure to assuage any other of your concerns.[2]

How can I deal with rumors that are damaging morale?

Facts, candor, and timeliness are the best antidotes to rumors. It is important that management be very candid and that it makes all the facts available to employees and others in a timely fashion. That can be done via Web sites, telephone call-ins, taped messages, memos, and so forth.

When managing a crisis, I may simply not have time to devote a great deal of effort to communicating with everyone who wants to know what is happening. How can I handle this?

When Disaster Destroys Communication Channels

People in the developed world take modern modes of electronic communications for granted. In fact, our dependence on fax machines, e-mail, the Internet, telephones, radio, and television to communicate with one another is enormous. We only appreciate that dependence during a power outage, or when our Internet service or company servers go down. These outages, fortunately, last only minutes in most cases.

Crisis managers must understand that major natural or man-made disasters can wipe out electronic links for days or weeks at a time, limiting their ability to communicate with employees and the public. This is exactly what happened in lower Manhattan during the 9/11 terrorist attack. The collapse of New York City's Twin Towers destroyed hundreds of thousand of land telephone lines, millions of data circuits, and key cell-phone systems. Even land mail was disrupted. The potential of a similar service disruption in your area should encourage you to devise a backup plan using nontraditional channels like these:

Take the time! Communications are absolutely critical in solving problems. And the best communications of all are face to face and from the person in charge. The next best option is to delegate this duty to a reliable and trusted officer of the company.

If I am required to speak to the media, should I speak off the record?

In general, it is a poor practice to speak off the record. If you don't want to see statements you are making in print, you probably shouldn't make those statements in the first place. On rare occasions, it may be helpful to provide background information, but that should be done only in extraordinary circumstances.

- Buy a page in the newspaper to get your message out.

- Use press interviews to spread news and instructions to employees.

- Find a way to get the CEO on a popular radio or TV talk show to explain what's happening.

- Route communications through a branch office in a city unaffected by the disruption.

Paul Argenti has described how American Airlines adapted its Sabre ticketing and flight information machines to communicate with its worldwide network of employees during the 9/11 crisis. With Sabre terminals in every American Airlines ticket counter and employee lounge, the system proved to be a handy and effective medium through which management could speak directly to employees about the crisis.[a]

[a]See Paul Argenti, "Crisis Communication: Lessons from 9/11," *Harvard Business Review*, December 2002, 103–109.

If I have important information to reveal relating to a crisis, whom should I tell first: the media, the employees, the shareholders, or the public?

All should be told at the same time. First of all, remember that information travels very quickly today. Tell one person about the crisis, and the story may be communicated around the world via e-mail and telephone. Given that each of your constituencies is extremely important and has a right to know, the only practical solution is to inform everyone at about the same time.

If I'm in charge of a geographically diverse team at the time of a crisis, should I return to headquarters, where I have good communications and staff support, or should I go to the location of the crisis?

The answer to this obviously depends on the circumstances, but it is generally best to be at the scene of the crisis. Being at the scene will put you in direct touch with the situation and its hour-to-hour evolution. It will also give everyone a clear message that you are concerned and in charge. If you need key headquarters staff to assist you, either bring them along or communicate with them via e-mail or telephone.

Should I ever state publicly how bad the eventual outcome of a given situation might be?

An effective leader cannot be a pessimist. By the same token, a good leader must be a realist. Most people, particularly employees, would rather know the full range of reasonable possibilities than to be surprised by a very negative outcome. By adopting a strategy of total candor, the possibility always exists for positive news—something that is welcome in times of crisis. Also, if you prepare people for the worst by stating the worse reasonably possible outcome, the chances are good that the actual outcome will be better than what most expected.

Should I publicly admit an error?

If an error has been made, the answer would generally be yes. There are, of course, legal implications to doing so that must be weighed. In the long term, however, it is best to recognize errors, if for no reason other than they will almost inevitably be discovered and made public. In the end, the public has more respect for people and organizations that admit their mistakes than for those who shrink from those mistakes.

Should the public spokesperson in times of crisis be the head of public relations?

The spokesperson should be the CEO if the crisis affects the corporation as a whole. Only the most senior individual can be broadly recognized as having authority to speak on behalf of the entire organization. For a crisis confined to an individual part of the corporation, the head of public relations may act as the organization's spokesperson.

Summing Up

- The media is one of the channels through which you will communicate with the public and company stakeholders, so be candid and accurate, and frame your messages as you'd like them reported. And give the media the facts that support your messages.

- Ignoring the media will not put a lid on the story. It will only encourage reporters to develop and frame the story as they see it—which might not be what you'd like.

- Before you meet with the media, do two things: (1) Anticipate the questions that news reporters are likely to ask, and (2) make a list of the five questions you would *least* like to be asked, and then be prepared to answer them.

- Treat reporters with respect in good times, and they're more likely to portray your company fairly in bad times.

- As you develop your communication strategy, begin with audience segmentation. Then develop messages that address the concerns of each segment. Finally, use the most appropriate media to reach each segment.

- Be prepared for the possibility that a physical disaster may disable your existing lines of electronic communications.

- The best time to develop a communication strategy is *before* a crisis occurs.

8

Learning from Your Experience

Gather Lessons Where
You Find Them

Key Topics Covered in This Chapter

- *Declaring the end of the crisis*

- *Building a document log from which people can learn*

- *Learning from crises and putting that learning to work*

WHEN A PERSON with money crosses paths with a person with experience, the experienced person usually comes away with the money, and the other person comes away with an experience. Something similar happens during an organizational crisis. Experience has a large price tag. Even the best-managed crisis can cost millions. Johnson & Johnson's experience in the Tylenol case probably cost it some $700 million (in 2003 dollars). But in return for its pain the company received the benefit of experience—if it was alert and eager to learn. And that experience may pay important future dividends. Consider these examples:[1]

- Measures adopted by World Trade Center tenants after the first band of terrorists set off a powerful car bomb in one of the towers' underground parking lots in 1993 are credited with saving many lives eight years later, when terrorists struck again.

- Hurricane Andrew hit Florida's coast in 1992, causing a record $16.8 billion in insurance claims—the highest recorded losses from a natural disaster in U.S. history. The unprecedented claims encouraged U.S. insurance companies to rethink their approach to risk-sharing and to find ways to reduce their exposure.

This chapter provides useful tips on closing down a crisis team. It also explains how you can learn from crises and use that learning to avoid and/or prepare for future situations.

Mark the End of the Crisis

At some point, someone in authority must declare that the crisis is over and that a crisis mind-set is no longer appropriate. That point is determined entirely by the circumstances. Here are a few examples:

- You've fended off a hostile takeover, or you've just been gobbled up by Predator Conglomerate, Inc. In either case, the crisis is over.

- The antimonopoly lawsuit that threatened to split your company into separate parts has failed, ending the crisis.

- The laptop computers that randomly burst into flames in people's briefcases have all been recalled and replaced with a safer model. End of crisis.

- The CEO has been found guilty of embezzlement and sentenced to three years in prison, where he will be teaching a course on business ethics. So ends an embarrassing chapter of company history.

Trials and tribulations eventually come to an end—for better or worse. The problem is resolved, and life returns to normal. Management must recognize and communicate this transition from crisis to normalcy.

Momentous events require a sense of closure, and business crises are no different. The organizational leader should provide such closure through a companywide meeting, a Web broadcast, or some other appropriate means. In a small or medium-sized company, the leader should visit every work group. Whichever the method, the leader should:

- Recap the crisis by explaining what happened and why it happened

- Provide a clear and candid picture of how things have been resolved; do not gloss over the losses or attempt to put a prettier face on the outcome than reality allows

- Let everyone know how things stand as of today

- Offer a plan for getting back to work and moving forward

- Remind people of the company's strategic goals

- Encourage everyone to do his or her best in moving forward

If the company has come out of its crisis without too much damage—or with a victory—consider some form of celebration: a catered lunch, a company outing, or an afternoon off for all employees. And be sure to thank the people who helped the company weather the storm. Celebrating, however, is not appropriate if anyone was hurt or killed during the crisis; a memorial service may be more suitable.

Record the Crisis Response

Every crisis produces a record. The value of documenting the crisis and the response was noted earlier. Depending on the situation, documentation might include:

- A notice of noncompliance from a government regulatory agency

- Test data on a product alleged to have caused harm

- The crisis action plan

- A log of actions taken

- Copies of press releases

- Newspaper clippings

- A list of crisis team members and other participants

- The minutes of the crisis management team's meetings

- A stack of paid invoices for costs incurred because of the crisis

- A formal after-action damage assessment

Those documents are part of the historical record; they should be collected and stored.

Why bother with documentation, especially when the whole company is eager to put the past behind it and get back to business? The reason is that documentation is a source of learning, and learning is what makes organizations stronger. Consider this example:

> *It has been six years since a major winter storm last paralyzed the town of Wyethburg, hometown of Technodigit Products. That storm caused a five-day closure of the company's office headquarters and manufacturing plant, resulting in lost revenues, severely delayed order fulfillment, and huge overtime costs in the weeks that followed.*
>
> *Today, Technodigit has a new cast of characters. Its CEO and many senior managers have been recruited from the outside, and few who helped manage the last snow crisis are still employed by the company. Institutional memory has faded with the years.*
>
> *With winter approaching, the company's chief operating officer is eager to prepare for the worst. Must he develop a crisis management plan from scratch? Fortunately, no. A secretary who worked for the COO's predecessor at the time of the last snow emergency has brought him some gratifying news. "We have a big file around here somewhere," she tells him. "Someone kept a record of everything that happened during the blizzard of '98. I'll try to find it."*
>
> *An hour later the secretary delivers a three-ring binder and a box of documents. It contained items that will make the COO's job easier, including the 1998 snow crisis action plan and a postmortem describing everything that worked well and worked poorly—with suggestions for plan improvement.*

The executive in this story was spared lots of hard work thanks to documentation done by an earlier crisis team. Best of all, he gained the experience of people who had faced a similar crisis in the same location. Your crisis team may likewise be a gold mine of useful information during future crises—but only if you gather together all important documents and store them in accessible formats.

Capture the Lessons Learned

Many companies spend thousands of people-hours on planning and millions of dollars on implementing but very little time reflecting on what they have done. They don't approach learning in a systematic way. Consequently, they lose much of the value that comes with experience. Not every organization is this shortsighted. The U.S. Army has maintained its Center for Army Lessons Learned for decades. The center's mission is to learn whatever it can from every type of combat operation and turn that learning into practical advice that it then disseminates to soldiers in the field. It actively solicits input from battle-tested soldiers on everything from urban warfare maneuvers, to when and when not to wear body armor, to the effectiveness of high-tech systems under adverse field conditions as experienced in mountainous Afghanistan.

The center also looks outside the army's own experience for important lessons. One article on its Web site, for example, documented and evaluated the tactics used by Chechen rebels in the embattled city of Grozny and the problems that Russian forces had in dealing with those insurgents.

Most businesspeople believe that they are light-years ahead of the military in matters of management. But lessons learned is one area in which private industry can learn a lesson of its own. And plenty of those lessons can be found in crisis management team operations and their supporting reports.

Lessons learned should be part of every crisis closedown operation. Participants should convene to identify what went right and what went wrong. This should happen as soon as possible after the crisis has passed, while memories are fresh. Participants should make a list of their successes, their failures, their unjustified assumptions, and things that could have been done better. That list should become part of the documented record.

Here is a partial list of questions that should be addressed at a lessons learned session:

- Given what we knew at the time, could the crisis have been avoided? How?

- What were the early warning signs of crisis?

- Could we have recognized the signs earlier? How?

- Which warning signals were ignored? Which were heeded? (Explain each response.)

- At what point did we realize that we faced a crisis?

- To what extent were we prepared with contingency plans or a crisis team?

- Did we have a solid plan, or did we rely on improvisation?

- Did we have the right people on the team? If not, who should have been included?

- What was the nature of our communications to different audiences? How effective were those communications?

- How effective was our public spokesperson?

- Was our leadership highly visible?

- Were our responses timely and adequate for the situation?

- What did we do right? What could we have done better?

- Which were our biggest mistakes?

- Knowing what we know now, how can we prevent the same type of crisis from occurring again?

- And the ultimate question: If we could replay this entire event, what would we do differently?

Those questions should not be asked to punish or to allocate blame, but to evaluate the performance of the response team and to prepare the organization for the future. Gather input from everyone who participated in a meaningful way. You need everyone's story, but pay particular attention to those people with expertise in the areas of importance.

Once you've gathered answers to those questions, draw out the lessons. Most should be obvious. Then record them in a systematic

TABLE 8-1

Lessons Learned: Blizzard of 2004 Plant Closing

	What Worked	What Didn't Work	Ways to Improve
Precrisis planning	• Had most of the right people on the team • Knew whom to call • Supervisors knew what to do	• Part of the weather emergency plan was outdated • Took too long to get organized • Waited too long to send people home because CEO could not be reached; result: many caught on snow-covered roads • Plan failed to include a snowplowing contract; result: all plows were busy when we most needed them.	• Update plan every six months • Contract for emergency snow-plows far in advance • Simulate a weather emergency each year • Empower COO or head of HR to act in CEO's absence
Warning signs	• Made decisions quickly once the blizzard potential was obvious	• Didn't check forecast hourly • Didn't notice that other businesses in town had already sent people home	• Pay closer attention to forecasts
Communi-cations	• Good communi-cations with employees; they knew when to leave and when to return	• Customers were left out of the loop; many could not get information on their orders for six days	• Put a self-serve order-status facility on the Web site • Refer customers to the site through the recorded emer-gency message

list grouped by topic (e.g., precrisis preparedness, warning signs, communications, execution, etc.) and organized in a form similar to table 8-1. Make this list available to all subsequent project teams.

Note: You can identify other lessons from your experience by using the "Worksheet for Capturing Crisis Learning" found in appendix A. It will help you break down the problems you faced, how you handled them, and what you learned. Using that information, you can figure out how to prevent a similar problem from reoccurring and/or how to respond to it more effectively.

Putting Learning to Work

Once you have drawn out the lessons of a crisis, integrate them with your plans and practices. One way to do that is to establish continuity within crisis-planning and crisis management teams. For example, if the company has just experienced a major fire, make sure that several veterans of that crisis are assigned to any subsequent crisis management team (assuming they have the right skills and performed well). These veterans will bring the experience of that earlier crisis with them and will be sources of knowledge for less experienced team members. This is the very same method used by airlines, which pair more experienced pilots with less experienced copilots.

Business crises are usually costly. Even in the best cases they throw a monkey wrench into operations and unsettle employees and customers. The worst cases can cost billions. The only good thing you can say is that they provide opportunities to learn. Make the most of these learning opportunities, and you may be able to avoid or better handle the next crisis that comes your way.

Summing Up

- The leader should provide closure to the crisis, thereby signaling that a state of normalcy has resumed. People need closure before they can move forward.

- Thank people for their help and their patience during the crisis. If the outcome was not too damaging, celebrate the crisis's end.

- Create a file of all materials relevant to the crisis. Documentation creates a record for future learning.

- At the end of the crisis, use an informal meeting to get people talking about what went right, what went wrong, and what could have been handled more effectively. Make a systematic list of these learning points.

Useful
Implementation Tools

This appendix contains a number of tools that can help you before, during, and after a crisis. All the forms are adapted from Harvard ManageMentor®, an online product of Harvard Business School Publishing.

1. **Emergency Contact List (figure A–1).** This form can be used as a contingency plan in some scenarios.

2. **30 Warning Signs of Potential Trouble (figure A–2).** Use this list to spot potential problems.

3. **Worksheet for Capturing Crisis Learning (figure A–3).** Use this form to capture some of the learning that you, your team, your division, or your company gleaned from experiencing the crisis.

Emergency Contact List

Name:				
Home Address:				
Work Phone	**Home Phone**	**Cell Phone**	**E-mail Address**	**FAX Number**

Name:				
Home Address:				
Work Phone	**Home Phone**	**Cell Phone**	**E-mail Address**	**FAX Number**

Name:				
Home Address:				
Work Phone	**Home Phone**	**Cell Phone**	**E-mail Address**	**FAX Number**

Name:				
Home Address:				
Work Phone	**Home Phone**	**Cell Phone**	**E-mail Address**	**FAX Number**

Name:				
Home Address:				
Work Phone	**Home Phone**	**Cell Phone**	**E-mail Address**	**FAX Number**

Name:				
Home Address:				
Work Phone	**Home Phone**	**Cell Phone**	**E-mail Address**	**FAX Number**

Name:				
Home Address:				
Work Phone	**Home Phone**	**Cell Phone**	**E-mail Address**	**FAX Number**

Additional Notes

Source: Harvard ManageMentor® on Crisis Management.

FIGURE A-2

30 Warning Signs of Potential Trouble

Questions	Yes	No
1. Is your company a start-up business?		
2. Is your group releasing a new product or launching a new service?		
3. Are you instituting a new process?		
4. Is your business in an area of rapid technological advancement?		
5. Has your company recently experienced a change in management?		
6. Has your department or the company just been through (or is it about to go through) a significant reorganization?		
7. Are your department's or company's profits declining?		
8. Is your company's business highly regulated?		
9. Does your business depend on a single product or service?		
10. Does your company depend on a few major suppliers?		
11. Does your company depend on a few (or one) major customers?		
12. Are your information technology systems weak?		
13. Has your company recently diversified into a new market or new location?		
14. Is the general attitude of your division or group arrogant, aggressive, and risk-taking?		
15. Do your business activities have the potential to harm the environment?		
16. Does your company lack successors for key employees or a transition plan?		
17. Has your department or company recently experienced rapid growth?		
18. Has your product or the company been experiencing declining market share?		
19. Is your company in litigation, or does it have disputes with outside auditors?		
20. Does your company depend on obscure financial statements and/or on *pro forma* accounting?		
21. Does your business depend on family relations or ownership?		
22. Is your company susceptible to natural disasters?		
23. Is your company's credit rating poor?		
24. Is your division or company experiencing high employee turnover or having difficulty retaining talent?		
25. Is your company vulnerable to fraud?		
26. Do you or does your company have high public visibility?		
27. Does your company's labor force have a negative relationship with management?		
28. Is your company operating in a politically or economically unstable country?		
29. Does your company have inadequate cash reserves?		
30. Does your department or company use hazardous materials or manufacture hazardous products?		

Totals _____

If you checked "yes" for:

15 or more	*Head for the bunkers!*	6–9	*You could be in trouble soon.*
10–14	*Your company's in trouble.*	5 or fewer	*Good score. Are you sure you're in business?*

Source: Adapted from "50 Warning Signs That Your Company May Be in Trouble" by Norman Augustine. Copyright 2002 Norman Augustine. Used with permission of the author.

Worksheet for Capturing Crisis Learning

Crisis or Problem	Action Taken	What We Learned	Preventative Action
Example: Key executive suddenly left to join another company.	We rushed into a disorganized search for a replacement.	We were unprepared and didn't know what our search criteria were. The process took too long.	Develop a succession plan for every key position in the company.

Summary

In what ways did we handle the crisis effectively? How can we be sure to incorporate these positive actions into our crisis management plans?

In what ways did we mishandle the crisis? What were the negative effects of our actions? How can we improve our crisis management in the future?

Source: Harvard ManageMentor® on Crisis Management.

How to Write
a Press Release

Companies write press releases (or news releases) when they wish to announce something significant to the general public: the launch of a new product, a product recall, a legal settlement, the departure of a senior executive, an important promotion, a plant closing, and so forth. Press releases are even used to communicate negative news, though always in a way most favorable to the company's public image. The press release is a tool that crisis managers can use to communicate with the general public.

In large companies, press releases are normally handled by the vice president of communications or by the corporate public relations staff. The managers of smaller companies must write and distribute their own press releases. If you are one of those small-company managers, consider these tips for writing press releases:

- Begin with an eye-catching headline to give readers the big picture and to generate interest.

- Make the message clear and concise—ideally less than one page in length.

- Develop the message around the five *W*s: who, what, where, why, and when.

- Try to capture all the important parts of your message within the first paragraph.

- Always include the name and phone number of a company representative whom the press can contact for more information.

Here's a prototype press release:

Gizmo Products, Ltd., 123 Millpond Boulevard
Mississauga, Ontario L5J 1K7, Canada
Telephone (905) 822-6015
Web site: http://www.gizmoproducts.on.ca

FOR IMMEDIATE RELEASE

MISSISSAUGA, ONTARIO. FEBRUARY 3, 2004. Gizmo Products
has announced the recall of 3,212 trash compactors built and distributed
by the company between November 2001 and March 2002. Though
no injuries have been reported, the company has discovered a manufacturing defect that could result in minor injuries if the product were
used in one of several unusual conditions. All recalled units are "Super
Cruncher Deluxe" models, and all were sold through distributorships
in Ontario and in the northeastern United States. They carry serial
numbers XCV-231 through XCW-547. Gizmo Products distributors
will manage the recall.

"We discovered the defect during our ongoing reliability-testing
process," according to Gizmo's CEO, Jane Pelletier. "And while it poses
no danger to anyone who operates the Super Cruncher according to
instructions, improper usage might result in the door opening quickly,
potentially bruising the operator."

Distributors of the recalled units will contact all customers with a
notice of the problem and an offer of a free exchange. The manufacturer
will share its product warranty registration data with the distributors
for purposes of the recall.

Mississauga-based Gizmo Products manufactures a full line of
household trash compactors, in-sink waste disposals, and pet-waste
products. Its self-cleaning cat litter box, EverClean®, was this year's
winner of the prestigious Better Mouse Trap Award of the Canadian
New Product Design Council (CNPDC).

For more information, contact Ian Beaton, Vice President
of Communications, at (905) 734-5321.
E-mail: ibeaton@gizmoproducts.ca.

Notes

Introduction

1. See Columbia Accident Investigation Board, *Report Volume 1*, 1 August 2003, 9. Obtainable at <http://www.caib.us/news/report/volume1/chapters.html>.

2. Ibid., 8.

3. Ibid., 181.

Chapter 1

1. As described to the writer by Laurence Barton, who was in charge of Motorola's crisis management at the time.

2. Ian I. Mitroff and Murat C. Alpaslan, "Preparing for Evil," *Harvard Business Review*, April 2003.

Chapter 2

1. Source of statistics: "Environmental, Social and Economic Sustainability," 3M Web site, <http://www.3m.com/about3m/sustainability/index.jhtml> (accessed 19 September 2003).

2. Susan Candiotti, "ValuJet 592 Crash to Be Blamed on Oxygen Canisters," CNN Interactive, 15 November 1996, <http://www.cnn.com/US/9611/15/valujet/index.html> (accessed 16 February 2004).

Chapter 3

1. The five steps listed here are adapted with permission from Harvard ManageMentor® on Crisis Management (Boston: Harvard Business School Publishing, 2002).

2. Steven Fink, *Crisis Management,* Backinprint.com Edition (Cincinnati: Authors Guild, 2002), 64.

Chapter 4

1. Carol Hymowitz, "Lessons Learned from Year's Blunders," *Wall Street Journal,* 16 December 2003.

2. Putnam was not the only practitioner of market timing. Investigations by state and federal regulators found many mutual fund companies guilty of the same practice. To its credit, Putnam's management acted quickly and forthrightly in admitting the problem, cooperating with federal and state regulators, fixing the problem, and communicating with its customers. It also fired fifteen employees and admonished others less culpable.

3. Norman R. Augustine, "Managing the Crisis You Tried to Prevent," *Harvard Business Review,* November–December 1995, 147–58.

4. See Gregory Watson, *Strategic Benchmarking* (New York: John Wiley & Sons, Inc., 1993), 129–48.

5. Augustine, "Managing the Crisis," 147–58.

6. Vincent P. Barabba and Gerald Zaltman, *Hearing the Voice of the Market* (Boston: Harvard Business School Press, 1991), 227–48.

Chapter 5

1. Laurence Barton, *Crisis in Organizations II* (Cincinnati: Southwestern College Publishing Company, 2001), 8.

2. Richard Boudreaux, "Putin Says He Will Take Complete Responsibility for Kursk Disaster," *Los Angeles Times,* 24 August 2000.

3. Barton, *Crisis,* 2.

Chapter 6

1. Paul Argenti, "Crisis Communication: Lessons from 9/11," *Harvard Business Review,* December 2002, 103–109.

2. Ibid., 103–109.

Chapter 7

1. Steven Fink, *Crisis Management,* Backinprint.com Edition (Cincinnati: Authors Guild, 2002), 90.

2. These questions and answers adapted with permission from Harvard ManageMentor on Crisis Management (Boston: Harvard Business School Publishing, 2002).

Chapter 8

1. Chris Zook and Darrell Rigby, "How to Think Strategically in a Recession," *Harvard Management Update,* November 2001, 8–9.

For Further Reading

Notes and Articles

Argenti, Paul. "Crisis Communication: Lessons from 9/11." *Harvard Business Review*, December 2002.

The sheer enormity of the terrorist attacks on the World Trade Center and the Pentagon disrupted established channels not only between businesses and customers but between businesses and employees. Internal crisis-communications strategies that could be quickly implemented were critically important. In this article, executives from a range of industries talk about how their companies, including Morgan Stanley, American Airlines, Verizon, and the *New York Times*, went about restoring operations and morale. From his interviews with these individuals, the author distills a number of lessons, each of which, he says, may "serve as guideposts for any company facing a crisis that undermines its employees' composure, confidence, or concentration."

Augustine, Norman R.. "Reshaping an Industry: Lockheed Martin's Survival Story." *Harvard Business Review*, November–December 1997.

In this behind-the-scenes story about the effects of the end of the Cold War on industry, Augustine draws important lessons about what industries can do to avoid crises and to manage them once they begin.

Dutton, Jane E., Peter Frost, Monica C. Worline, Jacoba M. Lilius, and Jason M. Kanov. "Leading in Times of Trauma." *Harvard Business Review*, January 2002.

Crises—the death of a beloved leader, a natural disaster that kills thousands—often cause emotional pain that spills into the work place, overwhelming employees. During these times, leaders must ease the collective anguish and confusion by unleashing a companywide, compassionate response. This article explains how. By demonstrating their own compassion, communicating company values, and using existing systems to mobilize needed resources, leaders help employees find meaning amid chaos and inspire action amid agony. Their companies can adapt, even excel, during difficult times.

127

Frost, Peter and Sandra Robinson. "The Toxic Handler: Organizational Hero—and Casualty." *Harvard Business Review,* July–August 1999.

> During times of crisis, when bitterness and confusion reign, a certain brand of manager quietly shoulders others' emotions, listens compassionately—and softens the company's collective pain. These "toxic handlers" save their companies from self-destructing during traumatic times. But their job is exhausting, and they risk burnout themselves. To keep your toxic handlers at their posts, you need to understand exactly what they do, show them you appreciate them—and help them stay healthy in their inherently unhealthy role.

Harvard Business School Publishing. "How to Keep a Crisis from Happening." *Harvard Management Update,* December 2000.

> This article focuses on Norman Augustine's first step to crisis management: prevention. Crisis prevention requires vigilance and mindfulness. The article offers these pointers: (1) Conduct regular crisis audits to identify organizational vulnerabilities that could turn into crises (e.g., numerous customer complaints could foreshadow a product recall); (2) solicit information from employees and customers—your best watchdogs; (3) benchmark your company against competitors to spot potential risks; and (4) don't let information you amass gather dust—put it to good use immediately.

Smith, N. Craig, Robert J. Thomas, and John A. Quelch. "A Strategic Approach to Product Recalls." *Harvard Business Review,* September–October 1996.

> Product recalls can destroy brands and entire organizations. But a company can ease the negative impact of a product recall—and even reap benefits. The authors offer step-by-step guidelines to handling a product recall, from the readiness stage, to sound recall management, to product reintroduction after the recall. For each stage, the authors explain what the policy and planning, product development, communications, and logistics and information systems functions should do. Well managed, a product recall can transform trouble into opportunity.

Books

Barton, Laurence. *Crisis in Organizations II.* Cincinnati: Southwestern College Publishing, 2001. This definitive and thorough work features issue-centric chapters and provides detailed research and practical advice on preventing and managing crisis. An analysis of more than fourteen hundred disasters allows the reader to benefit from the learning of those confronted with real crisis. The content on employee communications is particularly good.

Blythe, Bruce T. *Blindsided*. New York: Portfolio/Penguin Group, 2002.

Blythe's book covers the usual crisis management topics but also includes a number of immediate action steps for different types of incidents, such as accidental deaths in the work place, civil unrest, floods, biochemical exposure, and so forth.

Burrough, Bryan and John Helyar. *Barbarians at the Gate: The Fall of RJR Nabisco*. New York: HarperCollins, 1991.

This thoroughly researched story reveals how power, greed, and ego all combined to create a crisis. It's a business book that reads like a John Grisham novel. Not only will you learn about the dos and don'ts of crisis management, but you'll also learn what a leveraged buyout is. Laugh and learn at the same time.

Fink, Steven. *Crisis Management: Planning for the Inevitable*. Backinprint. com Edition. Cincinnati, Ohio: Authors Guild, 2002.

A well-written and practical treatment of crisis management. Using numerous case studies, Fink tracks the seeds of crisis, analyzing what mistakes were made and how the crisis was either exacerbated or contained by the decisions of management.

Grove, Andrew S. *Only the Paranoid Survive: How to Exploit the Crisis Points That Challenge Every Company*. New York: Bantam Books, 1999.

The cofounder and chairman of Intel Corporation shares his experiences with the ups and downs of Intel. He provides an inside look at the way change from every quarter can affect a major corporation, and he explains his vision for capitalizing on change and crisis in practical, direct language.

Harvard Business School Publishing. *"Harvard Business Review" on Crisis Management*. Boston: Harvard Business School Press, 1999.

This collection of eight essays highlights leading ideas on how to deal with difficult situations, crises, and other sensitive topics in a business environment. Obtaining the managerial skills and tools to effectively manage or avoid these crises is critical to the survival and success of your organization. In the lead article, "Managing the Crisis You Tried to Prevent," Norman Augustine uses his extensive personal experience in many executive situations to break down crises into predictable stages with advice on how to handle each one. Other articles in this compilation give practical advice from frontline people on such topics as layoffs, product recalls, executive defection, media policy, and leadership.

Hurst, David K. *Crisis and Renewal: Meeting the Challenge of Organizational Change*. Boston: Harvard Business School Press, 2002.

Hurst presents a radically different view of how organizations evolve and renew themselves. The author tracks a cross-section of enterprises from their creative beginnings through the institutionalization of their success. Using a model of organizational ecocycles, he argues that managers need to create deliberate crises to preserve their organizations from destruction and to renew them with creativity and meaning.

Mitroff, Ian I., Christine M. Pearson, and L. Katharine Harrington. *The Essential Guide to Managing Corporate Crises*. Oxford: Oxford University Press, 1996.

An analytic approach to crisis management, this book breaks down crises into identifiable types and uses decision trees, flow charts, and other diagrams to track the steps of planning for and managing a crisis. It provides valuable worksheets and other tools to help busy managers analyze potential risk in their organizations.

Silva, Michael and Terry McGann. *Overdrive: Managing in Crisis-Filled Times*. New York: John Wiley & Sons, Inc., 1995.

Using many case studies, the authors break down common myths about the best ways to handle crises and also pay special attention to how corporate cultures and leadership skills affect the outcome of a crisis.

Index

About the Subject Adviser

LARRY BARTON is president of The American College, a leader in financial services education based in Bryn Mawr, Pennsylvania, focused on the insurance and financial services industries. Dr. Barton began his career as a journalist, writing for the *Boston Globe, New York Times,* and other publications focusing on corporate debacles; that led to teaching management communications and crisis management at Harvard Business School, Boston College, and Penn State University from 1985 to 1995. Starting in 1987 he began consulting with major companies on crisis prevention and risk management, leading him to join Motorola as vice president of communications and public affairs, where he served from 1995 to 1999. Over the years he has consulted with Exxon Mobil, Disney, Honda, Nike, GoldStar of Korea, and the Japanese Ministry of Information, among many other assignments. He has managed more than three hundred serious incidents for these clients, including work-place murder and executive threats, embezzlement, product tampering, extortion, and various natural disasters.

Dr. Barton is the author of three books, including the best-selling *Crisis in Organizations II.* He is a frequent speaker at insurance and risk management forums on public perceptions of corporations during and after a high-profile incident. He has been featured in the *Wall Street Journal* and has been interviewed by the major global television networks regarding the effective management of crises.

About the Writer

RICHARD LUECKE is the writer of this and eleven other books in the Harvard Business Essentials series. Based in Salem, Massachusetts, Mr. Luecke has authored or developed more than thirty books and dozens of articles on a wide range of business subjects. He has an M.B.A. from the University of St. Thomas.

Harvard Business Review Paperback Series

The Harvard Business Review Paperback Series offers the best thinking on cutting-edge management ideas from the world's leading thinkers, researchers, and managers. Designed for leaders who believe in the power of ideas to change business, these books will be useful to managers at all levels of experience, but especially senior executives and general managers. In addition, this series is widely used in training and executive development programs.

Books are priced at $19.95 U.S.
Price subject to change.

Title	Product #
Harvard Business Review **Interviews with CEOs**	3294
Harvard Business Review on **Advances in Strategy**	8032
Harvard Business Review on	
Becoming a High Performance Manager	1296
Harvard Business Review on **Brand Management**	1445
Harvard Business Review on **Breakthrough Leadership**	8059
Harvard Business Review on **Breakthrough Thinking**	181X
Harvard Business Review on	
Building Personal and Organizational Resilience	2721
Harvard Business Review on **Business and the Environment**	2336
Harvard Business Review on **Change**	8842
Harvard Business Review on **Compensation**	701X
Harvard Business Review on **Corporate Ethics**	273X
Harvard Business Review on **Corporate Governance**	2379
Harvard Business Review on **Corporate Responsibility**	2748
Harvard Business Review on **Corporate Strategy**	1429
Harvard Business Review on **Crisis Management**	2352
Harvard Business Review on **Culture and Change**	8369
Harvard Business Review on	
Customer Relationship Management	6994
Harvard Business Review on **Decision Making**	5572
Harvard Business Review on **Effective Communication**	1437

Title	Product #
Harvard Business Review on **Entrepreneurship**	9105
Harvard Business Review on **Finding and Keeping the Best People**	5564
Harvard Business Review on **Innovation**	6145
Harvard Business Review on **Knowledge Management**	8818
Harvard Business Review on **Leadership**	8834
Harvard Business Review on **Leadership at the Top**	2756
Harvard Business Review on **Leading in Turbulent Times**	1806
Harvard Business Review on **Managing Diversity**	7001
Harvard Business Review on **Managing High-Tech Industries**	1828
Harvard Business Review on **Managing People**	9075
Harvard Business Review on **Managing the Value Chain**	2344
Harvard Business Review on **Managing Uncertainty**	9083
Harvard Business Review on **Managing Your Career**	1318
Harvard Business Review on **Marketing**	8040
Harvard Business Review on **Measuring Corporate Performance**	8826
Harvard Business Review on **Mergers and Acquisitions**	5556
Harvard Business Review on **Motivating People**	1326
Harvard Business Review on **Negotiation**	2360
Harvard Business Review on **Nonprofits**	9091
Harvard Business Review on **Organizational Learning**	6153
Harvard Business Review on **Strategic Alliances**	1334
Harvard Business Review on **Strategies for Growth**	8850
Harvard Business Review on **The Business Value of IT**	9121
Harvard Business Review on **The Innovative Enterprise**	130X
Harvard Business Review on **Turnarounds**	6366
Harvard Business Review on **What Makes a Leader**	6374
Harvard Business Review on **Work and Life Balance**	3286

Management Dilemmas:
Case Studies from the Pages of
Harvard Business Review

How often do you wish you could turn to a panel of experts to guide you through tough management situations? The Management Dilemmas series provides just that. Drawn from the pages of *Harvard Business Review,* each insightful volume poses several perplexing predicaments and shares the problem-solving wisdom of leading experts. Engagingly written, these solutions-oriented collections help managers make sound judgment calls when addressing everyday management dilemmas.

These books are priced at $19.95 U.S.
Price subject to change.

Harvard Business Essentials

In the fast-paced world of business today, everyone needs a personal resource—a place to go for advice, coaching, background information, or answers. The Harvard Business Essentials series fits the bill. Concise and straightforward, these books provide highly practical advice for readers at all levels of experience. Whether you are a new manager interested in expanding your skills or an experienced executive looking to stay on top, these solution-oriented books give you the reliable tips and tools you need to improve your performance and get the job done. Harvard Business Essentials titles will quickly become your constant companions and trusted guides.

These books are priced at $19.95 U.S., except as noted.
Price subject to change.

Title	Product #
Harvard Business Essentials: **Negotiation**	1113
Harvard Business Essentials: **Managing Creativity and Innovation**	1121
Harvard Business Essentials: **Managing Change and Transition**	8741
Harvard Business Essentials: **Hiring and Keeping the Best People**	875X
Harvard Business Essentials: **Finance**	8768
Harvard Business Essentials: **Business Communication**	113X
Harvard Business Essentials: **Manager's Toolkit ($24.95)**	2896
Harvard Business Essentials: **Managing Projects Large and Small**	3213
Harvard Business Essentials: **Creating Teams with an Edge**	290X
Harvard Business Essentials: **Entrepreneur's Toolkit**	4368
Harvard Business Essentials: **Coaching and Mentoring**	435X
Harvard Business Essentials: **Crisis Management**	4376

The Results-Driven Manager

The Results-Driven Manager series collects timely articles from *Harvard Management Update* and *Harvard Management Communication Letter* to help senior to middle managers sharpen their skills, increase their effectiveness, and gain a competitive edge. Presented in a concise, accessible format to save managers valuable time, these books offer authoritative insights and techniques for improving job performance and achieving immediate results.

These books are priced at $14.95 U.S.
Price subject to change.

Title	Product #
The Results-Driven Manager: **Face-to-Face Communications for Clarity and Impact**	3477
The Results-Driven Manager: **Managing Yourself for the Career You Want**	3469
The Results-Driven Manager: **Presentations That Persuade and Motivate**	3493
The Results-Driven Manager: **Teams That Click**	3507
The Results-Driven Manager: **Winning Negotiations That Preserve Relationships**	3485
The Results-Driven Manager: **Dealing with Difficult People**	6344
The Results-Driven Manager: **Taking Control of Your Time**	6352
The Results-Driven Manager: **Getting People on Board**	6360

Readers of the Harvard Business Essentials series find the following Harvard Business School Press books of interest.

If you find these books useful:	You may also like these:
Negotiation (1113)	HBR on Negotiation and Conflict Resolution (2360) RDM Winning Negotiations That Preserve Relationships (3485)
Managing Creativity and Innovation (1121)	Creativity, Inc. (2077) Code Name Ginger (6730)
Managing Change and Transition (8741)	Leading Change (7471) The First 90 Days (1105)
Hiring and Keeping the Best People (875X)	The War for Talent (4592)
Business Communication (113X)	Working the Room (8199)
Manager's Toolkit ($24.95) (2896)	Smart Choices (8575) The Balanced Scorecard (6513)
Creating Teams with an Edge (290X)	The Wisdom of Teams (3670) Leading Teams (3332)
Entrepreneur's Toolkit (4368)	The Entrepreneurial Mindset (8346)
Coaching and Mentoring (435X)	Results-Based Leadership (8710) The Art of Possibility (7706)

How to Order

Harvard Business School Press publications are available worldwide
from your local bookseller or online retailer.
You can also call

1-800-668-6780

Our product consultants are available to help you
8:00 a.m.–6:00 p.m., Monday–Friday, Eastern Time.
Outside the U.S. and Canada, call: 617-783-7450
Please call about special discounts for quantities greater than ten.

You can order online at

www.HBSPress.org

Need smart, actionable management advice?

Look no further than your desktop.

Harvard ManageMentor®, a popular online performance support tool from Harvard Business School Publishing, brings how-to guidance and advice to your desktop, ready when you need it, on a host of issues critical to your work. Now available in a PLUS version with audio-enhanced practice exercises.

Heading up a team? Resolving a conflict between employees? Preparing a make-or-break presentation for a client? Setting next year's budget? Harvard ManageMentor delivers practical advice, tips, and tools on over 30 topics right to your desktop–any time, just in time, and just in case you need it. Each topic includes:

1. Core Concepts: essential information in an easy-to-read format

2. Practical tips, tools, checklists, and planning worksheets

3. Interactive practice exercises and audio examples to enhance your learning

Try out two complimentary topics for Harvard ManageMentor® PLUS
by going to: **http://eLearning.harvardbusinessonline.org**

Harvard ManageMentor is available as a full online program with over 30 topics for $195 or as individual downloadable topics for $19.95 each. Selected topics are also available as printed Harvard ManageMentor Business Guides for $12.95 each and on CD-ROM (4 topics each) for only $49.95. For site license and volume discount pricing Call 800.795.5200 (outside the U.S. and Canada: 617.783.7888) or visit http://eLearning.harvardbusinessonline.org.

HARVARD
ManageMentor®
An online resource for
managers in a hurry